Behind Closed Doors

Also by Maggie Hartley

Behind Closed Doors

SUBTITLE TO COME

MAGGIE HARTLEY

SEVEN DIALS

First published in 2022 by Seven Dials,
an imprint of The Orion Publishing Group Ltd
Carmelite House, 50 Victoria Embankment,
London EC4Y 0DZ

An Hachette UK company

1 3 5 7 9 10 8 6 4 2

A CIP catalogue record for this book is
available from the British Library.

ISBN (Mass market paperback): 978 1 8418 8480 6
ISBN (eBook): 978 1 8418 8481 3

Typeset by Born Group
Printed and bound in Great Britain by Clays Ltd, Elcograf S.p.A.

www.orionbooks.co.uk

Dedication

This book is dedicated to Nancy, Sid and all the children and teenagers who have passed through my home. It's been a privilege to have cared for you and to be able to share your stories. And to the children who live with me now. Thank you for your determination, strength and joy and for sharing your lives with me.

Contents

A Message from Maggie   viii

ONE   *A Waiting Game*   1

TWO   *More Questions than Answers*   12

THREE   *The Worst News*   21

FOUR   *Secrets in the Penguin*   32

FIVE   *Missing Mummy*   44

SIX   *Lost and Found*   58

SEVEN   *The Truth Will Out*   69

EIGHT   *Behind Bars*   79

NINE   *School Days*   91

TEN   *Forward Planning*   104

ELEVEN   *Decisions*   116

TWELVE   *The Hardest Goodbye*   128

THIRTEEN	*A New Arrival*	138
FOURTEEN	*Concerns*	149
FIFTEEN	*The Terrible Truth*	156
SIXTEEN	*Difficult Conversations*	167
SEVENTEEN	*A Family Reunion*	180
EIGHTEEN	*Coming Home*	193
NINETEEN	*Facing the Future*	207
	Epilogue	219
	A Note from Maggie	221
	Acknowledgements	223

A Message from Maggie

I wanted to write this book to give people an honest account of what it's like to be a foster carer. To talk about some of the challenges that I face on a day-to-day basis and to talk about some of the children that I've helped.

My main concern throughout all this is to protect the children that have been in my care. For this reason, all names and identifying details have been changed, including my own, and no locations have been included. But I can assure you that all my stories are based on real-life cases told from my own experiences.

Being a foster carer is a privilege and I couldn't imagine doing anything else. My house is never quiet but I wouldn't have it any other way. I hope perhaps my stories will inspire other people to consider fostering as new carers are always desperately needed.

Maggie Hartley

CHAPTER ONE

A Waiting Game

I paced up and down the shiny floors for what felt like the umpteenth time, retracing my steps past the rows of uncomfortable plastic chairs and the out-of-order vending machine until I got to the double doors with the sign marked 'labour ward'.

I peered through the glass panels, desperate to know what was going on behind them, but they remained well and truly closed.

I glanced at my watch. Two hours earlier, I'd driven my heavily pregnant foster daughter, Louisa, and her husband, Charlie, to the hospital. By the time we'd got here, her contractions had been so strong I was worried she was going to give birth there and then in the back seat of my car. Thankfully a midwife had come to the rescue with a wheelchair and the last time I'd seen Louisa, she was being wheeled through these doors. Since then, I hadn't heard a peep.

No news is good news, I told myself over and over, desperately hoping that in this case it was true.

Occasionally the doors would open and I'd look up expecting to see a midwife or a doctor coming out. Then my heart would sink again as they walked straight past and I realised they weren't coming out to speak to me.

We already knew the baby was a girl but she was four weeks early and I knew Louisa was worried. It was understandable given everything that she'd been through. Over a year ago she'd given birth to a boy called Dominic. At the twenty-week scan, they'd found out he had abnormalities that meant he wouldn't survive, so heartbreakingly she'd had to be induced and gave birth to him before he died in her arms.

She'd been terrified when she'd got pregnant again a few months later. Even when regular scans showed the baby was healthy and growing fine, Louisa had never truly relaxed so I hoped and prayed that this time around everything was okay.

Just then my phone pinged with a text.

Any news yet?

It was my friend Vicky. She was a foster carer too and she'd known Louisa as long as I had. Louisa had come to live with me at the age of thirteen, after both her parents had tragically died in a car accident. I'd brought her up ever since and that scared, grief-stricken girl was now a strong, caring woman and I couldn't have been more proud of her than if I'd given birth to her myself. I knew she was going to make a brilliant mum and I just hoped everything was going well behind those double doors.

Still waiting. No news, I replied to Vicky.

I'd just put my phone back into my bag when the labour ward doors suddenly opened and a midwife walked out. I looked up and my heart started thumping as I realised that she was walking towards me.

'Maggie?' she asked.

2

'Yes,' I nodded, rising to my feet. 'Is everything OK? How's Louisa?'

'Come with me,' she smiled.

I quickly followed her through the double doors, down the corridor and into one of the rooms. Sitting up in the bed was an exhausted-looking Louisa. Her long dark hair was plastered to her forehead with sweat and her cheeks were flushed, but she had the biggest smile on her face. In her arms, wrapped in a blanket that I'd knitted, was a tiny but perfect baby girl. Charlie was sat by her side looking slightly shell-shocked but equally as happy.

'Come and meet your granddaughter, Maggie,' she grinned, beckoning me over.

Charlie stood up so I could sit down on the plastic chair next to the bed. I peered at her in amazement.

'Oh my goodness,' I gasped, my eyes filling with tears. 'She's absolutely beautiful.'

Tears of happiness and relief filled my eyes as I stroked her soft pink cheek.

'I'm so glad you're both OK,' I sighed. 'I was so worried.'

'She took a while to come out but Louisa was incredible, and the baby cried straight away once she was born,' smiled Charlie. 'She's five pounds, which the midwife said was a decent weight, even though she's early.'

'Have you given her a name yet?' I asked.

'She's called Edith Violet,' Louisa told me proudly. 'Edith was my mum's middle name after her grandma and Violet was Charlie's gran's name. We'll probably call her Edie for short.'

'That's beautiful,' I smiled.

'Would you like to hold her?' asked Louisa.

'Are you sure? I don't want to take her away from you.'

'Of course,' she grinned. 'One of the midwives is bringing me a cup of tea and some toast and I don't want to risk spilling it on her. I'm starving after all of that!'

Nervously, Charlie picked up Edie and gently placed her in my arms. She squirmed and squawked a little bit but then she quickly settled down again. I tucked the blanket around her and her tiny fist curled around my finger.

'Hello there, Edie,' I whispered. 'It's your nana here. We've been waiting such a long time to meet you.'

Louisa smiled.

As I held this tiny, perfect bundle in my arms, I was overwhelmed by such a strange mixture of feelings. I was overcome with happiness at meeting my granddaughter but at the same time I felt a real sense of sadness remembering baby Dominic and how I'd held him for the first and last time in this very same hospital. I knew Charlie and Louisa must be feeling exactly the same, but for now, we were all full of joy and relief that everything had turned out well and we had this gorgeous new addition to our family.

....

Six weeks later

I collapsed into a chair, exhausted, and admired my handiwork. I'd spent the past few days painting one of the bedrooms that I used for fostering. I wanted to keep it neutral so it would work for any child, regardless of their gender or age, but I'd given the walls a fresh coat of off-white paint and it looked much fresher and cleaner.

My whole body was aching now though. It was gone 10 p.m. and I'd been at it since this morning and I was totally and utterly wiped out. As I went downstairs to the kitchen to wash out my brushes, I was looking forward to sinking into a nice, hot bath before I headed to bed.

For the first time in as long I could remember, I'd had the past six weeks off. In all of the years that I'd been fostering, I'd never had more than a couple of weeks in between placements. But when my last foster child had left just before Louisa's due date, I'd asked my agency not to put me back on the vacancy list.

To be honest, I'd loved every minute of the past few weeks. I'd spent time with Louisa and helped her with Edie when Charlie had gone back to work. They were doing brilliantly and I'd loved getting to know my granddaughter and being able to be there for Louisa when she'd needed me. I'd also spent a bit of time with my boyfriend, Graham, a physiotherapist, and I'd spring-cleaned the house from top to bottom, sorted out the loft and decorated. All in all, it had been a lovely few weeks, I thought to myself as I turned the taps on for my bath.

I'd just got out of the bath and had padded downstairs in my dressing gown to get a quick glass of water before bed, when I heard my phone ringing from where it was charging in the kitchen. My heart sank. It was 11 p.m. In my experience, when your phone rings at that time of night then it's generally not good news. I ran to it, worried that it was Louisa and there was something wrong with Edie but it was a number I didn't recognise.

I managed to answer it just before it went to voicemail.

'Hi Maggie, it's Mary,' said a voice. Mary was one of the social workers from the fostering agency that I worked for. I'm sorry to bother you so late but I'm on duty tonight and I was really hoping you might be able to help me with an emergency placement that's just come in.'

'Oh, I'm not actually on the vacancy list at the moment,' I told her. 'I'm having a bit of time off.'

'I know, I realise that and I'm really sorry,' she sighed. 'I wouldn't ask if I wasn't desperate. I've been ringing round but there aren't any other carers who can help so I thought I would try you on the off-chance. I also think it's one of those cases where we need an experienced foster carer. It's really tragic . . .'

The local authority often used our agency to help them find foster carers for emergency placements when all of their carers were full.

I could hear the desperation in her voice and I had to ask what this was about. It was so late and my heart went out to any child or children that had to be taken into care at this time of night.

I took a deep breath.

'What's the situation?' I asked.

'Unfortunately, it's a really distressing case,' she sighed.

As she began to explain, I couldn't quite believe what I was hearing. I'd been a foster carer for many years but I'd never come across anything like this before.

Mary told me that she was calling from a hospital where she was with an eleven-year-old girl called Nancy.

'Earlier this evening, Nancy's next-door neighbour heard screaming,' she told me. 'She found Nancy on the street in her pyjamas, covered in blood and absolutely hysterical.'

Mary explained how the girl had led the neighbour into her house.

'That's where she found him,' sighed Mary.

'Found who?' I asked.

'Nancy's dad Martin,' she told me. 'He was lying on the kitchen floor with a knife stuck in his side.'

'What?' I gasped. 'That's awful.'

'He was bleeding profusely and was losing consciousness.'

What had followed sounded like utter chaos. The neighbour had called the emergency services and had stayed with a hysterical Nancy by his side until Martin had been taken away to hospital and the police had arrived.

'What on earth had happened to him?' I asked. 'Who stabbed him? Where's Nancy's mum?'

'At this point, no one really knows,' Mary sighed. 'The police are still trying to piece it all together.'

She explained that, according to the neighbours, Nancy's mum, Helen, also lived at the house but she had gone missing. There was no sign of a burglary or forced entry.

Martin had been rushed to hospital and was currently undergoing emergency surgery to stop his internal bleeding. Nancy had been taken to hospital too to be checked over.

'How is she?' I asked, my heart in my throat.

'Well, thankfully she's not injured,' sighed Mary. 'The blood she was soaked in was all from her dad.'

The poor, poor girl. I couldn't even imagine how frightening that must have been for her.

'Has she said anything about what happened?' I asked Mary.

'That's the thing,' she told me. 'She literally hasn't said a word since the neighbour found her. She was hysterical at first and now she's just silent.'

I wasn't surprised. I knew that shock and trauma could do that to people, especially a child.

'The police have been to the hospital to speak to her because obviously they want to try to find out where her mum is and to get her account of what happened and who could have done this but she wouldn't say anything – she just stared into space.'

'The poor girl,' I sighed.

'All they know from what they've pieced together from the neighbours is that there's no sign of Helen; she's not answering her phone and her car has gone. The police have put out alerts to try to find her so they can question her.'

It was horrific. It sounded like something from a TV drama or a film, not real life.

'And how's her dad?' I asked.

'We don't know yet,' she sighed. 'It's touch and go. He's lost so much blood and they think the knife perforated some of his organs.'

Awful.

The hospital had said that medically Nancy was fine and so there was no need to keep her in overnight, so Social Services had to find somewhere for her to go. When they couldn't find anybody, they'd called my agency and spoken to Mary.

'I'm here at the hospital with Debbie – the social worker from Social Services,' she explained. 'She's liaising with the police so I offered to ring round our carers and try to find somewhere that Nancy can go.

'It's late, she's exhausted and in shock and I just want to find a safe place for her but it's proving quite difficult,' she sighed. 'If we get desperate then the hospital may let her stay here but I didn't want to leave her on her own on a noisy ward after everything she's been through tonight.'

The other option was a children's home but that would feel overwhelming for a child who had just been through such a traumatic ordeal. She needed one-to-one care after everything she'd been through tonight.

My heart went out to her. What on earth had happened in that house? What horrors had she seen?

'She can come here,' I said firmly. 'That poor child has been through enough.'

'Are you sure?' asked Mary.

'Yes,' I told her. 'I want to help.'

'Oh thank you so, so much, Maggie,' sighed Mary. 'I know you're not working at the moment but she just needs a safe place to go while the police find out more and we know how Martin is.'

She explained that the police were going to try to question Nancy one more time to see if they could find out any more information.

'They're being as gentle as they can with her but they do need to know where her mum is and try and get a sense of what happened to Martin,' she told me. 'Debbie is with her at the moment but she's busy making calls, so as soon as the hospital discharges her, I'll bring Nancy round to you. I know it's late but it might be another hour or so.'

'That's OK,' I told her. 'I'll be up and waiting for you.'

'Thank you,' sighed Mary. 'And if anything changes then I'll keep you posted. Thanks again, Maggie.'

'I'm happy to help,' I told her. 'I'm happy to help.'

But, as I put the phone down, I wondered what on earth I had just agreed to take on.

I went back upstairs and got changed. Thankfully I'd decorated the smaller bedroom that I used for fostering a couple of weeks ago so that was all ready, down to fresh bedding on the single bed. I went into the huge cupboard on my landing and got out some clean towels, a flannel and a toothbrush. Luckily, I had a pair of age twelve pyjamas that I'd recently picked up in a sale so I put those on the bed too. They might be a little bit big for her but she could roll up the sleeves and the bottoms. Then I went downstairs and filled up a hot water bottle, which I put in the bed to make it nice and warm. Even though it was early summer, it was a chilly night and after everything Nancy had been through, I wanted everything to be as warm and comforting as possible.

I closed the curtains and put on the little lamp in the corner so it looked cosy. Then I went back downstairs and made myself a cup of tea.

All I could do now was wait and I didn't know how long they were going to be. I sat at the kitchen table with my laptop and started a logbook, filling it in with all the information that I knew about Nancy so far. Even writing it down, it was still so hard to get my head around it, especially as there were so many unanswered questions.

My phone pinged with a text and disturbed my thoughts. I thought it might be Mary with an update, but it was Louisa.

Are you still up? Just feeding Edie x

She often texted me when she was doing a late feed as she knew I was a bit of a night owl.

Yep I'm here, I typed. *Waiting for a new placement to arrive.*

An 11-year-old girl. Will tell you more when I see you.

Ooh exciting. Me and Edie might have to go for a walk tomorrow and pop in. Good luck x

I think I might need it, I thought to myself, as I looked at the logbook in front of me.

CHAPTER TWO

More Questions than Answers

I was deep in the middle of a dream when I felt something vibrating next to my head. My eyes flickered sleepily as I slowly came round and realised that I'd nodded off at the kitchen table. In a panic, I reached for my phone to see the screen lit up with a text.

Maggie, it's Mary. I'm outside. Are you there?

It was 1 a.m.

Quickly I jumped up and pulled my dressing gown around me. As I walked into the hallway, I heard a gentle tapping on the front door.

'I'm coming,' I mumbled as I rushed to open it, smoothing down my hair. 'I'm so sorry.'

A tall woman with blonde hair who I assumed was Mary was standing on the doorstep but there was no sign of any child with her. She showed me her ID and gave me a warm smile.

'Don't worry, Maggie,' she told me. 'I'm sorry it's so late. It took longer than I thought for the hospital to discharge her and the police had a few more questions.'

I looked around in the darkness but I could see she was on her own.

'Where's Nancy?' I asked, confused.

'She's in the car,' she told me. 'She's absolutely shattered, bless her. I just wanted to have a quick word with you before I brought her in.'

Mary explained that the police had questioned her again but she still wasn't saying anything.

'After everything she's been through tonight, we don't want to push her any more. I think the main aim now is to get her to bed, then the police and Social Services will try talking to her again in the morning.'

'How's her dad doing?' I asked.

'Martin was still in surgery when we left the hospital,' she sighed. 'They've promised to keep me updated so I'll let you know.'

'And her mum?'

'Still no sign,' she shrugged. 'There are so many unanswered questions about what went on in that house tonight but the main thing is Nancy's safe and she might feel like talking more tomorrow if she gets some rest.'

'I'll go to the car and bring her in,' she told me. 'I'm afraid all she's wearing is a hospital gown and a pair of my old trainers because her pyjamas were in such a state. They were absolutely soaked in blood.'

Even the thought of all that blood made me shudder and I couldn't imagine what it must have been like for such a young child to have actually seen it.

'The police have taken the pyjamas just in case they need them as evidence.'

'OK,' I nodded. 'I've got some clean ones for her upstairs and I can get some clothes together for her tomorrow.'

'Great,' she told me. 'Thank you, Maggie. I really appreciate you doing this with so little notice.'

'It's not a problem,' I told her.

And it wasn't. I desperately wanted to help Nancy after everything she'd been through.

'Right, I'll go and bring her in,' she sighed.

I watched nervously as Mary walked down the front path towards a small blue car. She opened the back passenger door and helped a girl out of the back.

Mary put her arm around her and guided her towards me. As she walked through the darkness towards the light of the hallway, I could see her properly for the first time.

She was tall for her age and slender with dainty features and long, poker-straight brown hair. She was in a flimsy hospital gown with a tatty blue hospital blanket draped around her shoulders.

'Hello lovey,' I smiled. 'You must be Nancy. I'm Maggie. Come on in.'

She looked up at me with glassy, expressionless brown eyes.

'Let's go through to the kitchen and I can get you a drink and a snack if you're hungry?'

Nancy didn't say a word and stared at me blankly. It was as if she was in a daze. Was she even registering what I was saying?

Mary guided her through to the kitchen and sat her down on one of the chairs. In the brightness of the kitchen lights, I noticed that she had brown marks down the side of her face and dark, sticky patches in her hair. I realised with horror that they were splatters of blood. *Her dad's blood.*

I could tell that she was in deep shock and incapable of answering any questions. Most children who are taken into care suddenly experience an element of shock and it can take many forms. Some can be incredibly aggressive and angry, others talk non-stop about the most random of things. Some are just completely silent, like Nancy was tonight. Everyone copes with trauma in different ways and after what she'd witnessed, it wasn't surprising that she wasn't communicating with us.

'There's a drink for you here if you want one, flower,' I said to her, putting a glass of water down on the table. She didn't say a word but she reached out for it. And as she lifted it to her mouth, I could see her fingernails were encrusted with dried blood too.

'Nancy, it's really late so I'm going to go in a minute,' Mary told her. 'You're going to stay here with Maggie tonight and then in the morning you'll meet your new social worker from Social Services.'

Nancy didn't react and I wasn't sure if she was taking any of it in.

'The hospital is going to keep me and Social Services updated about how your dad's doing so we'll let Maggie know when we have any news.'

Nancy stared blankly into space.

'I'm just going to see Mary out and then I'll show you your bedroom,' I told her. 'I'll be back in a minute.'

We walked out into the hallway.

'The poor kid's in shock,' I sighed. 'It's like her whole body has just shut down.'

'Hopefully she'll feel a bit better in the morning after some rest,' Mary replied. 'She must be exhausted and terrified, poor little mite. If she does say anything about where her mum might be or what happened, then please let me know and I can tell the police and Social Services. I'll leave my phone on overnight and you've got my phone number.'

'Thank you,' I said. 'I'll wait to hear from Social Services in the morning.'

'I'll email Becky and let her know what's happened too,' Mary replied.

Becky was my supervising social worker from the fostering agency and Mary's colleague.

After I'd said goodbye to Mary, I went back into the kitchen where Nancy was still sitting at the table staring into space.

'I'm going to take you upstairs now and show you your bedroom, flower,' I told her.

I cupped her shoulders and gently guided her upstairs.

'This is the room where you'll be sleeping,' I told her, leading her into the single bedroom. 'I've just decorated it so it's all lovely and fresh. There's a new pair of pyjamas on the bed, and a dressing gown, so get undressed and put the dressing gown on and I'll go and run you a nice bath.'

Even though it was almost 2 a.m. by now, I couldn't bear to send her to bed covered in her dad's blood and I hoped the warm water would help soothe and comfort her a little bit.

I went into the bathroom to start running the bath. When I came back into the bedroom, Nancy was standing in exactly the same spot that I'd left her in.

Even though I was a complete stranger to her, I could see that she was in such deep shock that I was going to have to undress her myself. She didn't object as I gently took off the hospital gown. I talked her through everything I was doing

16

but it was like undressing a ghost – she had a faraway look in her eyes like she wasn't really there.

Underneath the hospital gown, all she was wearing was a pair of knickers.

'Can you lift up your leg for me, sweetheart, so I can get these pants off?' I asked her.

I was relieved when she did as I'd asked. At least somewhere in there she was aware of what was happening.

I put a dressing gown around her shoulders so she wouldn't be cold and led her to the bathroom where I helped her into the bath. She didn't resist and sat down obediently in the water.

'I'm just going to wet your hair and give it a wash,' I told her.

As I massaged shampoo into her scalp, I could see the flecks of dried blood coming off into the bath water. Then I gently washed her face with a flannel and scrubbed her nails.

'Come on then, poppet, let's get you out of here and into those clean pyjamas, ready for bed,' I told her, pulling the plug out and reaching for a towel.

Suddenly Nancy glanced down at the bath water and a look of horror flashed across her face. I realised the bath water was now tinged a dark, reddish-brown colour because of all the blood that had washed off her. She burst into hysterical sobs.

I quickly grabbed the towel and wrapped it around her shoulders. Then I crouched down next to her and held her while she cried her heart out.

'It's OK, lovey,' I soothed. 'It's OK. You let it all out.'

She sobbed and sobbed, her little body shaking as all the fear and distress came tumbling to the surface.

I held her like that until all the water had drained away and she was sitting in an empty bath. I pulled the towel tighter around her as I could see she was starting to shiver and I helped her out of the bath. I wanted her to be warm but it was also important for her to acknowledge how she was feeling and I didn't want to rush her. When her sobs started to subside, I gave her hand a squeeze.

'Come on, sweetie, let's get you into bed,' I told her gently. 'You must be absolutely exhausted.'

She nodded her head, snivelling. After that she didn't say anything at all, and I didn't push her. Even though it was very late, I couldn't send her to bed with wet hair. So, after she'd got her pyjamas on, I sat her on a stool and quickly dried her hair with a hairdryer. Then I pulled the duvet down on the bed.

'You lie down now, lovey, and try to get some rest,' I told her. 'Your bed should be nice and warm as I put a hot water bottle in it.'

While she got into bed, I got a spare throw from my room and put it over the duvet and tucked it tightly in down both sides of the bed. I hoped that it would help give her a sense of security and make her feel safe. I'd used this technique many times before to help calm children down.

I reminded her again that my name was Maggie, just in case she hadn't taken it in when Mary had first introduced us.

'If you get upset in the night or you feel scared or you need anything, then you just yell for me,' I told her. 'My bedroom is just down the landing and I'll be right here, OK?

'Would you like me to stay with you for a little bit while you try to get to sleep?'

Nancy looked up at me with those blank brown eyes and

nodded. I turned the main light off and left the lamp on in the corner then I went and sat down on the end of her bed.

'I'm right here,' I soothed. 'You're safe now, sweetie. Just close your eyes and try to get some rest.'

I wanted her to know that I was there and that she wasn't alone.

She did as I'd asked and she closed her eyes and curled up. After a while I could hear her breathing get slower and deeper and I could see her body finally starting to relax as it gave in to sleep. I was so relieved that she'd managed to settle.

I sat there for fifteen minutes or so, then I got up and crept across the room. I didn't want her to be scared or distressed if she woke up and was confused, so I left the night light on, the door slightly ajar, and the light on the landing on.

As I wandered downstairs, my heart felt heavy. All I could think about was the poor little girl upstairs who had come to me in the most horrific of circumstances.

By now I was exhausted too but there was no way I could sleep. My mind was racing and the adrenaline of the past few hours was still flowing. I sat at the kitchen table and recorded everything that had just happened in an email that I sent to Becky, my supervising social worker at the agency. I knew Social Services would appoint Nancy a permanent social worker first thing in the morning.

I wasn't sure if I was going to face an unsettled night ahead of me. I hoped Nancy would manage a few hours' sleep but after all of the trauma she'd been through, it wouldn't surprise me if she was restless and woke up upset or in a panic. I couldn't even begin to imagine what she was going through. Her dad was fighting for his life in hospital, her mum was missing and she had been sent to stay at a stranger's house. There were so many questions about what had happened in that house tonight, but for now what Nancy needed most was sleep.

CHAPTER THREE

The Worst News

To my relief, Nancy slept through the whole night but the same wasn't true for me. As I'd feared, I couldn't settle, and tossed and turned for hours, lying there jumping at every sound, until I saw the light seeping in through the gap in the curtains. I was so tired but my mind was churning, wondering what the day ahead was going to bring and worrying about how Nancy was going to cope with it all.

Just after 6 a.m., I gave up trying to sleep and went downstairs to make myself a cup of tea and brought it back up to bed. Half an hour later, I heard rustling and movement coming from Nancy's room. I quickly put my dressing gown on, walked down the landing and gently opened her bedroom door. She was sitting up in bed, a puzzled look on her face. After everything that had happened last night, I thought she might be confused.

'Good morning,' I smiled. 'Do you remember that my name's Maggie and you came to my house last night after you'd been to hospital?'

'Yes,' she nodded.

'It was very late when you got to bed but I'm so pleased that you managed to get some sleep. Shall we go downstairs and get some breakfast?'

Nancy didn't reply but slowly she got out of bed and I handed her a dressing gown, which she put on.

'What kind of cereal do you like?' I asked her as we went downstairs. 'Or perhaps you'd prefer a boiled egg and some toast?'

She shrugged her shoulders. She was probably still in shock so I stopped myself from bombarding her with any more questions. Everything that had happened last night had been so sudden, and in reality, I was still a complete stranger to her.

I pulled out a chair and she sat down at the table and I put a few boxes of cereal out so she could choose which one she liked. Then I made a plate of toast and put some butter, jam and orange juice out so she could help herself.

'Please may I have some of these?' she asked, pointing to the box of cornflakes.

It was the first proper thing that she'd said to me. Her voice was soft and she was very well spoken.

'Of course you can, lovey,' I smiled, delighted that she'd finally said something. 'No need to ask.'

She poured herself a bowl and I passed her some milk.

'May I have some orange juice?' she asked.

'Yes,' I told her and poured some into a glass for her. 'Help yourself to anything that you fancy.'

She sat there while I spread some butter on a piece of toast.

'What is it, flower?' I asked her.

'Please may I start now?' she asked me.

I realised that she was waiting for my permission before she picked up her spoon.

'Of course,' I told her. 'Go ahead and tuck in. You must be starving.'

She was the most polite and most well-mannered eleven-year-old I'd ever come across.

'Your new social worker should be calling me this morning and then she'll probably want to come round and meet you,' I explained to her. 'Do you know what a social worker is?'

Nancy shook her head.

'While you're staying at my house, you have somebody that looks after you and makes sure that you're OK.'

Nancy looked confused.

'But I don't need that person,' she told me. 'My mummy looks after me.'

'Sweetheart, we're not really sure where your mummy is at the moment,' I replied. I paused, unsure whether to ask her the question that was on the tip of my tongue.

'Nancy, do you know where your mummy is?' I asked. 'The police would really like to talk to her and make sure that she's OK.'

Nancy looked down, shook her head and carried on eating her cereal. I didn't want to push her any more as I was sure there would be many more questions to come later in the day.

I was putting some more bread in the toaster when my mobile rang.

'I'm just going to get this as it might be Social Services,' I told Nancy. 'Excuse me for a minute.'

I went into the living room so I could talk without Nancy overhearing.

'Hello?' I asked.

A woman's voice told me that her name was Juliet and she explained that she was going to be Nancy's social worker.

'I'm just reading an email from my colleague and catching up with what happened last night,' she told me. 'It sounds horrific. How's Nancy doing?'

'As well as can be expected, given what she's been through,' I sighed. 'I was worried she wouldn't settle but she managed to sleep for a few hours, which is good, but she's still very quiet and subdued, but that's understandable. Do we know if her mum has turned up yet or how her dad is?' I added. 'I'm sure she will ask me.'

'I've only just come into the office so I don't know yet, I'm afraid,' replied Juliet. 'I'm about to call the police and the hospital now for an update.'

She promised to ring me straight back and let me know.

Suddenly I heard a flicker on the line.

'In fact that's someone trying to get through to me now,' Juliet told me. 'I'm going to take this, Maggie, and I'll call you straight back.'

Before I could reply, she'd hung up.

I was just about to go back into the kitchen when my mobile rang again.

'Hello Maggie, it's me again.'

The change in tone of Juliet's voice made my blood run cold and I could tell instantly that something terrible had happened.

'What is it?' I asked her.

'That was the police calling,' she told me. 'It's Nancy's dad, Martin. The doctors did their best, but I'm afraid he didn't make it. He died in the early hours of this morning.'

I could hardly take it in as she explained how the knife had perforated his internal organs and he'd lost too much blood.

'The police are now treating this as a murder inquiry,' she told me. 'They've issued national alerts to try to find Nancy's mother, Helen.'

All I could think about was Nancy and how she was going to take the news. Even though I hardly knew her, my heart ached for her.

'What happens now?' I asked.

'I need to come round and tell Nancy,' sighed Juliet. 'The police have asked if an officer can come with me because they want to ask her a few more questions about her mum and where she might be. They're hoping she might be a bit more forthcoming than last night. Has she asked about her dad at all?'

'No,' I sighed. 'Not yet. She didn't say a word last night and she's been very quiet so far this morning.'

'Before you rang, she did ask about her mum though.'

It was all such a mess and all I could think about was the eleven-year-old girl sitting in my kitchen whose world was about to be shattered.

'Do they honestly think her mum could have done this?' I asked.

'I don't think anyone knows for sure,' sighed Juliet. 'The police said there was no sign of a forced entry; Helen's mobile phone and her purse don't seem to be in the house so they say there's no suggestion that she was taken away against her will but they've got to look at every possibility.'

She explained that the police were going door-to-door and questioning neighbours to see if they had seen or heard anything last night.

'When do you want to come round and tell Nancy about her dad?' I asked.

'As soon as I can,' she replied. 'She needs to know.'

We agreed that she would give us an hour so Nancy had time to finish her breakfast and we could both have a shower and get ready. As I hung up the phone, my heart felt heavy. We were about to shatter a child's world and I was dreading it.

When I came back into the kitchen, Nancy looked up at me expectantly.

'Was that Mummy? Is she coming to get me?'

My heart sank.

'No sweetie, that was your new social worker,' I told her. 'It's a lady called Juliet and she's going to come round in a little while to talk to you.'

'I don't really want to talk to her,' she sighed.

'I know you don't, lovey, but she wants to introduce herself to you and she sounds very nice,' I reassured her.

She pushed her bowl of cereal away.

'I've finished, thank you,' she told me politely.

I felt so sorry for her and at a loss as to what to say. I spent the next hour on tenterhooks. I hated knowing something that I had to keep from a child, especially when it was something so distressing, but I knew I had to wait for her social worker. It was Juliet's job to tell Nancy what had happened to her dad, not mine, and I didn't envy her task one bit.

All I could do was get Nancy as ready as I could before the bombshell was dropped. She didn't want a shower, which I wasn't too bothered about as she'd had a bath the night before. I'd managed to find a few clothes in my cupboard that were Nancy's age, but she didn't seem impressed with the jeans and couple of tops that I'd picked up in the sale at ASDA a while ago.

'They're brand new,' I told her. 'And we can go to the shops later today if you want and pick up a few more bits.'

'But why can't I have my own clothes?' she asked. 'Please can I go home and get them?'

'Well that might not be possible lovey,' I told her. 'But we can ask Juliet about it when she comes.'

'Why?' she sighed. 'It's my house.'

I didn't want to tell her that her house was now a crime scene and that forensics were probably in there turning the place upside down.

'We'll see,' I smiled. 'Now you get yourself dressed as Juliet will be here soon.'

As I showered, I felt sick to my stomach knowing that we were getting closer to the time when Juliet and the police would arrive.

We'd just gone downstairs when there was a knock at the door. Nancy looked at me, terrified.

'That will be Juliet,' I told her. 'You go into the kitchen, lovey, and I'll bring her through.'

Nancy did as I asked and I opened the door to find two women in their thirties on the doorstep. One of them, a tall woman with long dreadlocks down her back, held out her hand to me.

'Nice to meet you, Maggie,' she smiled. 'I'm Juliet, and this is DC Hayley Hirst,' she said, gesturing to the red-haired woman next to her.

I was glad it was a female officer and that she wasn't in uniform so it wouldn't be as intimidating for Nancy.

'How's Nancy doing?' Hayley asked as I showed them in.

'As well as can be expected,' I told her. 'She slept and she managed to eat but she's still very shocked about what happened. She's in the kitchen so I'll take you through to her.'

Nancy looked terrified as we all walked into the room. Juliet introduced herself and Hayley while I put the kettle on.

'I'm your new social worker, so it's my job to make sure that you're OK and help to look after you while you're at Maggie's house.'

'I know,' she nodded. 'Maggie told me that.'

'And Hayley's a police officer and she's here to ask you a few more questions if that's OK so we can try to find out more about what happened last night.'

'Where's my mummy?' asked Nancy.

'I'm afraid we don't know that yet,' Hayley told her. 'But everyone is looking for her and hopefully we can find her very soon. That's why I wanted to talk to you to see if you've got any ideas about where she might have gone.'

'Is my daddy still in the hospital?' Nancy asked as I carried a tray of mugs back to the table.

I saw Hayley and Juliet exchange glances as I sat down next to Nancy.

'Nancy, I'm afraid I've got some really sad news,' Juliet told her.

As she began to speak, I put my arm around Nancy and gave her shoulder a comforting squeeze.

'Your dad was very badly hurt. The doctors tried everything they could to save him but I'm afraid he was too poorly and this morning he died.'

Nancy looked at her blankly then she looked at me.

'That's not true is it, Maggie?' she asked desperately.

'I'm so sorry, flower, but I'm afraid it is,' I told her.

As the news slowly sank in, she burst into tears.

'It's OK,' I told her, giving her a hug. 'You let it all out.'

She buried her head in my shoulder and sobbed. It was distressing to see a child so distraught and knowing there was nothing we could do to take away her pain.

Suddenly she pulled away from me.

'I want Mummy,' she whimpered.

Juliet got up from her chair, went over and crouched beside her.

'I know you do, darling,' she sighed, patting her hand. 'And this must be so hard for you but we don't know where your mummy is at the moment. As soon as we do then we'll do our best to let you see her.'

Nancy let out another whimper and buried her head back into my shoulder. She stayed like that for a little while, softly weeping, while I stroked her hair. Eventually her tears stopped and she pulled away from me.

'Nancy, I know you're very upset but it's really important that we find out what happened to your daddy and where your mummy is,' Hayley told her. 'So I need to ask you a few questions just in case you can help us. Is that okay?'

Nancy nodded.

'Did your parents have one car or two?'

'Two,' she sniffled. 'Daddy has a black one and Mummy's is the little red one.'

'Does your mum's family live nearby?' Hayley asked. 'Can you think of anyone she might have gone to stay with?'

Nancy shook her head.

'Mummy's family live a long way away in France so we don't ever see them,' she told us.

'What about friends?' asked Hayley. 'What are the names of Mummy's friends?'

'I don't know,' shrugged Nancy.

'Is there a place Mummy liked to visit?' asked Juliet.

'She sometimes goes to Sainsbury's,' replied Nancy.

I could tell Hayley was starting to get frustrated.

'What about last night?' she asked her. 'Where were you when your daddy got hurt?'

'In bed,' she said. 'Asleep.'

'Did something wake you up?'

She nodded again.

'What was it?'

Nancy shrugged.

'I can't remember. I think I heard the door bang or a car. I don't know what it was but I went down the stairs to find Mummy and get a drink of water.'

'And did you find her?' asked Hayley.

Nancy shook her head.

'What did you find?'

Nancy bit her lip and looked down at the ground then she burst into tears again.

'Daddy was in the kitchen,' her voice trembled as she continued. 'He was lying on the floor with all the red blood around him.'

'You're being so brave,' I told her, giving her hand a squeeze.

'You poor thing,' sighed Hayley. 'That must have been so scary for you. Could you see what had hurt him?' she asked.

Nancy nodded.

'He had a knife sticking out there,' she shuddered, pointing to her side. 'The big one that Mummy uses to chop the roast chicken.'

'What did you do then?'

'I ran out and screamed for Mummy.'

'And did she come?'

Nancy shook her head.

'She wasn't there,' she sighed. 'I looked and looked in all of the rooms but I couldn't find her.'

She let out a whimper.

'Maybe a bad person broke in and hurt Daddy?' Nancy sighed. 'But what if he hurt Mummy? What if she's dead too?'

Her sobs became more hysterical and I rubbed her back to try to calm her down.

I was relieved when Juliet stepped in.

'I think that's enough questions for now,' she sighed as Nancy collapsed, exhausted, into my arms.

CHAPTER FOUR

Secrets in the Penguin

It wasn't even 10.30 a.m. and Juliet and Hayley had left; Nancy just looked utterly exhausted. She seemed so helpless and scared and my heart went out to her. I desperately wanted to comfort her in any way that I could but we'd only known each other for a few hours.

'Do you want to go for a lie down in your bedroom?' I suggested but she shook her head.

'Would you like a drink?' I asked.

'No, thank you.'

'How about you help me wash up the breakfast dishes?' I asked. 'I'll wash, you can dry?'

'OK,' she nodded.

I didn't know what to do for the best but I thought giving her a job to do might help to distract her. Nancy hardly said a word as she dried the dishes but I didn't push her to talk.

We'd just finished when there was a knock at the door. Nancy glanced up at me with a worried look on her face.

'I'll go and see who it is,' I told her.

When I opened the door, I was surprised to see Louisa standing there with the pram.

'Oh hello lovey,' I mumbled. 'Is everything OK?'

'You've forgotten, haven't you?' she smiled. 'Remember I've got my six-week check at the doctor's and you said you'd look after Edie for me? Don't worry, I can take her with me if it's a bad time?' she added.

'Oh, er no,' I replied. 'My head's a bit all over the place today. I had a new placement arrive last night so it's been a bit hectic to say the least.'

'Oh no, it's me that's the forgetful one,' she sighed. 'You told me that when I texted last night. Edie was up half the night so I can't even think straight.'

Just then Nancy wandered into the hallway. She gasped when she saw the pram and she rushed over to it.

'Oh she's so tiny and cute,' she cooed.'

'Nancy, this is Louisa,' I told her. 'And you've already met baby Edie.'

'How old is she?' Nancy asked.

'Nearly seven weeks,' Louisa told her. 'Do you like babies?' Nancy nodded her head eagerly.

'Please may I hold her?' she asked Louisa.

'Well, let them come in first then you can have a chat to Louisa about that,' I said.

'I can wheel the pram,' Nancy told us.

We watched as she carefully pushed it into the hallway and through to the kitchen.

'I'm sorry, Maggie,' Louisa said in a hushed tone. 'We can go. I completely forgot you had a new child arriving.'

'No, it's fine,' I told her. 'Nancy had some really sad news this morning and I think Edie is providing a welcome distraction.'

I wouldn't normally have visitors or arrange to see anyone on a child's first day with me, especially after the traumatic news that she'd been told less than an hour before. But she seemed enthralled with Edie and maybe the baby was exactly what she needed to take her mind off things.

'Are you totally sure this is OK?' asked Louisa. 'I shouldn't be long.'

'Of course,' I smiled. 'I think Nancy will be delighted.'

Nancy had cried a lot after she'd been told about her dad's death and I was sure there would be many more tears to come, but for now, she was calm.

'You get off to your appointment,' I told her. 'Edie will be absolutely fine.'

'OK,' she said. 'She's just been fed but there's a bottle in the bag if she needs it and some nappies.'

I went back into the kitchen where Nancy was still cooing over Edie in her pram.

'Would you like to hold her?' I asked her and she nodded eagerly.

She sat on the floor and carefully I put Edie into her arms. She was very gentle with her and listened to what I told her about supporting her head.

I got a play mat out of the cupboard and we laid Edie down on it, and I got out a few rattles and a black-and-white-patterned cloth book.

'Babies of Edie's age can only see things in black and white,' I explained and I showed her how to stick her tongue out to see if Edie could copy her.

Nancy listened intently to everything I told her and she was very gentle.

'Gosh, you're very good with her,' I told her. 'Do you know any babies?'

'Rosie, my friend at school has a new baby sister called Ava,' she told me. 'She's a bit bigger than Edie and she's so cute.'

'When you go round to Rosie's house do you like playing with Ava?' I asked.

Nancy shook her head sadly.

'No, Daddy doesn't like me going to other people's houses.'

'Does Rosie come to your house?'

'No,' she said matter-of-factly. 'Daddy doesn't like that. He just likes it to be me and Mummy at home.'

Nancy helped me to change Edie's nappy, then we put her down in her pram for a sleep. Louisa was back within an hour.

'How's Edie been?' she asked.

'Absolutely fine,' I said. 'Nancy has been a superstar and she's looked after her brilliantly.'

Nancy nodded proudly.

'Do you want to go and watch some TV in the living room while I have a quick cup of tea with Louisa?' I suggested to her.

'Please may I go to the toilet first?' she asked me.

'Of course you can,' I replied. 'You can go to the loo whenever you need to, lovey, you don't need my permission.'

'What a lovely girl,' smiled Louisa when she'd gone out of the room. 'She's so well mannered.'

'She really is,' I agreed.

Louisa understood about fostering and children's confidentiality so she knew not to ask me any questions about why Nancy was with me and what had happened to her. She knew that I would tell her in my own time if I wanted to or if I thought it was appropriate.

'So was everything OK at the doctor's?' I asked her.

'Yes, all fine,' she said. 'She said I'm recovering well and my stomach muscles have knotted back together.'

We were chatting away when suddenly we heard a blood-curdling scream from the front room.

Louisa and I looked at each other in horror.

'Nancy!' I yelled, leaping up off my chair. 'Are you OK? What is it?'

I ran into the living room to find Nancy pointing at the television screen with a horrified look on her face.

'That's my house,' she sobbed, tears streaming down her cheeks. 'Why is my house on the TV?'

A male news reporter in a suit and tie was standing outside a huge detached house. The large black wrought-iron gates behind him were open and there was a forensic team in white suits bringing things in and out and a police officer stood guarding the front door.

'Police are appealing for information after the death of a forty-five-year-old man. Martin Miller was found stabbed last night and died in hospital in the early hours of this morning from his injuries . . . Detectives are hoping to trace his wife, Helen Miller, who has not been seen since the incident, which police say they're now treating as a murder inquiry.'

Nancy started screaming hysterically.

'No,' she shouted. 'They've got it wrong. They've got it wrong.'

I lunged for the remote control and quickly turned it off. I wasn't trying to hide anything from her but I could see Nancy was upset, and I kicked myself for not thinking about the news.

'Why were they talking about Mummy and Daddy on the TV?' she sobbed. 'Why are they saying he was murdered?'

Louisa looked shocked.

'I think I'll go and check if Edie's OK in the kitchen,' she mumbled.

I sat down with Nancy on the sofa and put my hand on hers.

'It's OK,' I told her. 'I know this is really hard for you and you must have so many questions.'

'Why are they saying my daddy has been murdered?' she asked me. 'That lady this morning said he'd died.'

The truth was brutal but I had to be honest with her.

'Your daddy died from his injuries and now the police need to find out who caused those injuries and why,' I told her. 'I know it must be very scary for you and really difficult to get your head around.'

Nancy curled up into a ball and started to cry.

'I want Mummy,' she sobbed. 'Where's my mummy? I want her to come now.'

'I know you do, Nancy, but we still don't know where your mummy is,' I soothed. 'The police are doing their best to find her and when they do, I'm sure they can arrange for you to see her.'

Nancy seemed to accept that and slowly she started to calm down. A few minutes later, Louisa popped her head around the door.

'I think I'm going to take Edie home now,' she told me.

I left Nancy on the sofa and I went to see her out.

'Sorry about that, flower,' I told her. 'Things are really hard for Nancy right now.'

'I can see that,' she sighed. 'I hope she's OK.'

After she'd gone, I went back into the living room. Nancy seemed a bit calmer. I didn't want to risk her seeing anything else on the news so I put a DVD on for her instead and went into the kitchen to make us some lunch. I was buttering some bread when my mobile rang. It was Juliet.

'How's Nancy?' she asked.

I explained what had just happened with the TV.

'You weren't to know, Maggie,' she told me. 'It's probably going to be all over the newspapers as well.'

She told me that the police had given her permission to go to the house and collect some of Nancy's things.

'It's still a crime scene but forensics are mainly working downstairs so I'm allowed to go straight to Nancy's bedroom with an officer and grab a few bits. I can drop them straight over to you if you'd like?'

'I think that would be a good idea,' I told her.

I thought it would help make Nancy feel more settled to have some of her own things around her and to be able to wear her own clothes. I didn't tell her that Juliet was going to her house as I thought she might ask to go too, and it would upset her again if she wasn't allowed.

At lunchtime, Nancy pushed her plate away and wouldn't eat more than a couple of mouthfuls of her sandwich.

'I'm sorry, Maggie, I'm not hungry,' she told me. 'My tummy hurts and I feel sick.'

'Don't worry,' I smiled, giving her hand a pat. 'Why don't you go for a lie down in your bedroom? You look really tired and it might help make you feel better.'

'I think I will,' she said.

I gave the kitchen a quick tidy and fifteen minutes later, I went to check on her.

I gently pushed open her bedroom door. Nancy was curled up in a ball on top of her duvet, fast asleep. She'd had such terrible news today and her poor body and mind must have been overwhelmed.

'Oh bless her,' I sighed to myself.

She was still asleep an hour later when Juliet arrived. She had a huge black suitcase with her that was bulging at the seams.

'Come in,' I told her. 'I'm glad you managed to get some of her things.'

I explained that Nancy was having a sleep.

'She was out like a light,' I sighed. 'I think the poor girl is just wiped out.'

We went through to the kitchen and I made us both a cup of tea.

'What was the house like?' I asked her. 'I saw it briefly on the news report.'

'Massive,' replied Juliet. 'And absolutely immaculate. It's like something out of a magazine, Maggie. Honestly, everything was gleaming and looked brand new.'

She described Nancy's bedroom to me. It was huge with sugar-pink walls, a four-poster bed, a dressing table filled with all kinds of jewellery and a whole wall of wardrobes that were full of clothes.

'It's like the perfect little girl's bedroom,' she sighed. 'I can see that she wanted for nothing.'

It sounded so different from the homes that the majority of the children that I fostered came from.

'I didn't have long because forensics weren't too happy about me being there but I managed to grab a few clothes and her school uniform, as well as a couple of cuddly toys that she had on her bed that I thought might bring her some comfort.'

'School was one of the things I was going to ask you about,' I told her. 'How do you think we should play it?'

Juliet said that from the look of Nancy's uniform, she guessed she went to one of the local private schools.

'I'll contact them today,' she told me. 'When they know what's happened, I'm sure they won't be expecting her back for a while. We also need to find out where her parents were up to with the fees.'

I knew there was no way Social Services would be able to pay private school fees so it would depend on what her parents had already paid.

'I think the police will probably want to interview Nancy again at some point,' Juliet told me.

'But she's already answered their questions at the hospital and this morning,' I sighed. 'Surely she's told them everything she knows.'

'I think they want to get it on tape while it's still fresh in her mind,' she told me. 'They might need it for evidence in the future or in case there's ever a trial.'

I nodded but as I took it all in, I asked the question that had been on my mind since last night.

'Do they really think her mother did this?'

Juliet shrugged.

'I only know the very little that the police have told me but it really does look that way,' she sighed. 'They say there's no sign of a forced entry, and the house had security systems in place. They'll know more when they've done all the forensics but so far they're saying nothing points to anyone else being in the house at the time.'

'But why?' I asked.

Why would a woman with what seemed like the perfect home and family suddenly want to stab her husband?

'Who knows?' asked Juliet. 'I don't think anyone knows enough about them at the moment.'

All I could do was focus on my immediate concern, which was Nancy.

'I feel so sorry for Nancy and how she's going to cope with all this,' I sighed. She was so fragile and only just starting to grieve for her dad. 'I worry about how she'll handle answering any more questions.'

'The police know she's been through a lot in the past twenty-four hours, so DC Hayley will do the interview and she'll be really gentle with her. I'll keep you posted when I know when it will be.'

After Juliet had left, I wheeled the suitcase into the kitchen. I'd just unzipped it and was about to go through it when a bleary-eyed Nancy came wandering in.

'Hi lovey,' I smiled. 'How are you feeling after your nap?'

'OK,' she sighed.

Her eyes focused on the open suitcase.

'Oh, that's my dress!' she gasped, running to the suitcase and getting down on her knees.

'Yes, the police said Juliet could go round to your house and get some of your things,' I told her. 'She brought them round while you were asleep.'

'But why did she go and not me?' she asked. 'I wanted to go to my house. Was Mummy there?'

I explained that the police had sealed off the house and only Juliet was allowed in with special permission.

'I'm afraid your mum wasn't there,' I told her. 'But the

41

police will tell you as soon as there's any news.'

'Why don't we go upstairs and I'll help you unpack your things,' I told her, quickly changing the subject.

I carried the case up to her bedroom and laid it on the bed.

Nancy started lifting some of the clothes out. Juliet had packed it all really neatly and the clothes were beautiful.

'You've got some lovely things,' I told Nancy.

She nodded.

'Yes, Daddy chose them,' she told me. 'He likes me to look smart.'

'You haven't even worn some of these,' I said, as I noticed a couple of pairs of tracksuit bottoms and T-shirts with the tags still on.

'Mummy chose those for me but Daddy didn't like them so I didn't ever wear them,' she said.

'Oh dear, that's a shame,' I replied.

Juliet had also put in a couple of cuddly toys. One was a stuffed penguin and the other was a toy dog that looked like it had seen better days.

'Oh it's Digby,' gasped Nancy, cuddling the dog to her.

'Is that your favourite?' I smiled.

'Yes, I've had him since I was a tiny baby,' she sighed. 'He always sits on my bed.'

'What about Mr Penguin?' I asked. 'Does he sit on your bed too?'

Nancy nodded. She picked up the penguin and gave it a squeeze. She had a panicked look on her face as she started pressing on its fur.

'What is it?' I asked her.

'Nothing,' she said, but I could tell there was something

wrong as she frantically ran her hand up and down the back of the penguin. I could see the seam was ripped and she stuck her hand into the stuffing.

'Oh no,' she gasped. 'It's gone.'

Her brow furrowed with worry.

'What's gone?' I asked her. What is it?'

'Mummy's secret money,' she sighed. 'It's gone.'

CHAPTER FIVE

Missing Mummy

Puzzled, I could see the panic on Nancy's face as she frantically searched through the stuffing inside the soft toy penguin.

'Secret money sounds very exciting,' I said casually. 'Why did your mummy have that?'

'Because she was saving up to buy Daddy a present and she didn't want him to find it,' she told me. 'She hid it in my penguin because she said he'd never look in there.'

'Had Mummy saved up a lot?' I asked.

Nancy nodded.

'She'd been doing it for a very long time,' she replied. 'There was a big roll of money. She's going to be really angry with me when she finds out it's gone. But it wasn't my fault – I promise I didn't take it.'

Suddenly she paused. She looked up at me and I could see her eyes were filled with tears.

'But it doesn't even matter now, does it?' she sighed sadly. 'Daddy isn't ever going to get his present.'

Tears began to roll down her cheeks and I wrapped my arms around her. Even though we hardly knew each other, I could see that she needed the comfort of a hug.

'It's OK, sweetie,' I soothed. 'It's all right. You let it all out.'

As her little body shook with sobs, my mind whirred into action about the missing money. Why would someone hide the money for a present in a child's stuffed toy? Had Helen taken it? I didn't know any of the answers but it felt significant enough for me to tell Juliet about it.

Eventually, Nancy's tears subsided and I got her a tissue.

'Are you OK?' I asked her, wiping away a stray bit of hair that was clinging to her wet cheek and tucking it behind her ear.

'I think so,' she sniffed.

'I just need to pop downstairs and make a quick phone call,' I told her. 'Do you want to come with me or shall I leave you to unpack some of your things?'

'I can unpack,' she nodded.

I got my mobile and went down to the kitchen to call Juliet and tell her about the missing money.

'I just wanted to let you know in case it's important,' I told her.

'You did the right thing, Maggie,' she replied. 'I'll phone Hayley now. She might want to call you if she's got any more questions.'

'That's absolutely fine,' I replied.

I went back upstairs to check on Nancy, who seemed engrossed in unpacking. There was a pile of perfectly folded clothes on the bed and she'd already hung the rest on hangers in the wardrobe.

'Wow,' I gasped. 'You're doing an amazing job.'

'Was your wardrobe as organised as this at home?'

'Yes,' nodded Nancy. 'Daddy liked things to be neat and tidy and I always kept my room clean.'

'Well I wish all the children I looked after were like you,' I smiled.

Just as I wandered back downstairs, my phone rang again. It was DC Hirst.

'Thanks for passing on the info about the missing cash,' she told me. 'Juliet just called me.'

'That's OK,' I told her. 'I'm not sure whether it means anything or not but I thought I should let you know.'

'Well to be honest we don't know either, but it could be that Helen has taken it with her, so it's useful to know as we're trying to build up a picture of where she might be. She hasn't used any of her bank cards, which was concerning us, but if she's got this cash then that might explain why.'

They clearly still hadn't managed to locate her.

'I wanted to talk to you about something else too,' Hayley added. 'We'd like to bring Nancy into the station so we can take a proper witness statement. We'd record it and we'd do it in a special interview suite that we use for minors and other vulnerable victims or witnesses.'

'OK,' I said. 'When were you thinking?'

'Do you think she's in the right frame of mind to bring her down this afternoon?'

'Today?' I gasped. 'I think that would be way too much.'

Nancy had only been told that her dad had died this morning and she was still in shock. I appreciated that they wanted to talk to her while things were still fresh in her mind and get it on tape but it hadn't even been twenty-four hours since he'd been stabbed.

'She's been very tearful today and I'm about to sort her some dinner soon,' I told her. 'I know you're thinking in terms of evidence, but my priority is Nancy's welfare and she's absolutely exhausted emotionally and physically.'

'I completely understand,' she replied. 'Could we try for tomorrow then?'

'I think that would be better,' I agreed. 'Hopefully she'll feel stronger if she manages another night's sleep.'

I completely understood that they were keen to talk to Nancy again more formally in case she had some information that might give them a clue as to where Helen might be.

'Are you allowed to tell me how the investigation's going?' I asked her.

She described how her team was doing door-to-door inquiries in the street.

'We're talking to Martin's work colleagues and trying to trace any immediate family.'

Helen was French and they'd found out she had a mother and father in France, as Nancy had told us, but she hadn't been in touch with them for several years.

'We're just trying to get hold of them now,' she told me. 'Martin's parents are both dead and he's got a brother who he's estranged from.'

Martin was a lot older than Helen – he was forty-five and she was thirty-one. A neighbour had said she'd told her they'd met when she'd come to England at nineteen to work as an au pair and she had never returned home.

'All the neighbours have described them as very nice and polite,' Hayley told me. 'They kept themselves to themselves but they seemed to have everything – big house, which they own outright, luxury holidays, new cars, private schooling. Neither of them have so much as a parking ticket to their name and the police have never been called to their home address. It's all just baffling. On paper, they seem like the perfect family.'

Helen didn't work and Martin was the CEO of an IT company that he'd founded.

'We've spoken to his business partner who was equally as glowing about him. Described him as a devoted dad and husband who liked nothing more than spending time with his wife and daughter. Helen's a quiet lady but lovely apparently,' she sighed. 'It's all just a complete and utter mystery at this point.'

It was all so puzzling. What on earth had happened in that house to lead to this tragic chain of events?

'Is there any way Nancy could be right and someone else came in and hurt her dad?' I asked.

'At this stage, none of the evidence suggests that but we're keeping an open mind,' she replied. 'Our priority now is to find Helen and make sure that she's safe.'

For Nancy's sake, I really and truly hoped that she was, as the alternative was just unthinkable.

The rest of the evening passed in a blur. Nancy didn't say much and hardly ate any dinner.

'You look shattered, love,' I told her. 'Let me run you a nice bath.'

She was in bed by 8 p.m. and thankfully was almost already asleep by the time her head hit the pillow.

It was so hard; none of us knew how or why this had happened or where her mum was, so I couldn't reassure her.

Thankfully Nancy had another settled night. I, on the other hand, tossed and turned for hours, going over everything in my mind and worrying about what the looming day was going to bring.

In the morning, I knew I had to broach the subject of a police interview with Nancy. It was something that had to be done so perhaps it was best just to get it out of the way.

'But the police lady's already asked me loads of questions,' she sighed. 'I've told her what happened.'

'I know, flower,' I told her. 'And I can't even begin to imagine how hard this is for you and how sad and scared you must be feeling. But Hayley only wants to talk to you so she can try to help you. She really, really wants to find your mummy and you might know something that will help her to do that. And she also needs to find out who hurt your daddy. So she's asking you all these questions for a good reason, OK?'

Nancy nodded. Everything was still so raw and anytime I mentioned her dad, I could see the pain and upset on her face.

'Why do we have to go to the police station?' she asked me in the car on the way there. 'Why can't she talk to me at your house like she did yesterday?'

'Because what you say might turn out to be really important so they want to record it,' I told her.

'What do you mean?' she asked, puzzled.

49

'Hayley will explain it all when we get there but some-times when people answer the police's questions they film it,' I told her. 'But don't worry, the cameras are really tiny and you won't even know that they're there. It's so they can remember everything that you tell them.'

Juliet was meeting us at a police station I'd never been to before, which was in a town around a forty-five-minute drive away from my house. She was already waiting for us in the car park with Hayley when we pulled up.

'Hi Nancy,' smiled Juliet. 'How are you doing today?'

'OK,' she sighed.

'I'm going to take us through the back entrance,' Hayley told us.

I was relieved, as police station reception areas were noto-rious for being crowded and full of angry or upset people and I didn't want Nancy to feel scared or intimidated.

'I'm going to take you through to a special room and then I'll explain what will happen,' she told Nancy before turning to me. 'Maggie, I'm afraid only Juliet will be allowed in the interview suite as Nancy's appropriate adult.'

'That's absolutely fine,' I nodded. 'I understand.'

Over the years, I'd taken several children to be interviewed at a safe house so I knew the protocol. To ensure that there was no risk of me being accused of influencing a child, it was procedure that I would always wait in another room while they were being questioned. At the safe house I could watch what was going on via a screen linked up in another room but I wasn't sure they had that facility here.

'One of my colleagues will take you to wait in another inter-view room and we'll give you a shout when we're finished.'

'No problem,' I told her but I could see the look of panic on Nancy's face.

'No!' she yelled, suddenly grabbing my hand and holding on to it with a vice-like grip. 'I want Maggie to stay with me. Why can't she stay with me?'

She'd been with me less than forty-eight hours but out of everyone there, she'd spent the most time with me.

'I'm happy for Maggie to stay if you are,' shrugged Juliet to Hayley. 'She's experienced enough to know not to interfere with the interview or coerce Nancy in any way.'

'Oh gosh, absolutely,' I said. 'I'm happy to sit at the back of the room and just observe.'

'Please,' begged Nancy. 'I won't talk to you if you don't let her stay with me.'

'Let me go and run it by my Detective Inspector,' said Hayley.

She went off and Juliet talked to Nancy.

'I know this is all really strange for you but we have to do what Hayley says,' she reassured her. 'She's a really nice lady and she just wants the best for you.'

Before Nancy could reply, Hayley came hurrying back down the corridor.

'OK,' she said. 'We don't normally allow it but as you weren't involved in the incident or connected to the case, my boss is happy for you to sit and observe. It will have to be at a distance though. You can't sit with Nancy.'

'Will that be OK, lovey?' I asked her and she nodded uncertainly, looking terrified.

Hayley led us down a warren of corridors until finally we got to the interview suite. I walked in and looked around. I could tell they were trying to make it more cosy so it felt more welcoming than a normal interview room, but the furniture was all worn and mismatched and it looked like it had been cobbled together from charity shops. There were copies of famous paintings on the walls in heavy gilt frames, a three-piece suite in pink Dralon with tassels on the bottom and a pine coffee table. Down the side of one wall was a teak sixties' sideboard with a plastic kettle and some polystyrene cups on top of it as well as a wicker basket filled with packets of crisps and biscuits.

'Nancy, would you like something to eat or drink?' Hayley asked her.

'No, thank you,' she answered politely.

Juliet made the rest of us a cup of tea while Hayley talked Nancy through what was going to happen. Hayley showed Nancy the cameras and explained that they would be recording her so they could remember what she said.

'I'm just going to check all the equipment before we start,' Hayley told us.

'You'll be fine, lovey,' I told Nancy, giving her hand a reassuring squeeze. 'All the police want to do is find out what happened to your dad and make sure your mum is safe, which I'm sure is what you want too.'

Nancy nodded.

'I'm going to sit over there,' I said, pointing to an office chair at the back of the room behind where she was sitting. 'But I'll be right here if you need me.'

She gave me a weak smile.

'OK then,' smiled Hayley. 'Let's get started then shall we? For the purpose of the camera, I'm going to introduce everyone in the room.

'Nancy, if you need a break or you want a drink or to go to the loo, just let me know OK?'

Nancy nodded.

I could see she was nervous but I knew Hayley would do her best to make her feel at ease and Juliet was there to reassure her too.

First they talked about what had happened earlier on the day of the stabbing when Nancy had come home from school.

'Mummy came to get me in the car like she always did,' she said. 'I practised piano and watched TV. Then Mummy made dinner.'

'Is Mummy a good cook?' asked Hayley, and Nancy smiled and nodded her head.

'Can you remember what you had?' she asked.

I could see she was doing her best to make Nancy feel at ease. She screwed up her face in concentration.

'I think we had lasagne,' she replied. 'Yes we did, because that's Daddy's favourite.'

The rest of the evening sounded very ordinary. Nancy described how Helen had cleared up after dinner, she'd played swing ball in the garden for a bit then they'd all watched TV and Nancy had gone to bed.

'How were your mummy and daddy when you went to bed?' Hayley asked. 'Were they in a good mood?'

Nancy shrugged.

'They were just like normal,' she said.

Nancy described how Helen had tucked her in like she always did, she'd read her book for a bit then Martin had come in, said goodnight and turned her light off.

'Can you remember what time that was?' asked Hayley.

'About nine, maybe?' suggested Nancy. 'I always go to sleep at that time.'

'Can you remember if it was still light outside?'

'Yes, I think it was a bit,' Nancy nodded.

Now came the difficult questions as Hayley got Nancy to recall what had happened later on that night. She remembered everything exactly as she had the day before. Some sort of loud noise had woken her up and confused and half asleep, she'd wandered downstairs and into the kitchen.

'Nancy, I know this must be so hard for you but please can you tell me exactly what you saw in the kitchen?' Hayley urged.

Tears filled Nancy's eyes.

'I saw Daddy,' she said, her voice wobbling with emotion.

'And what was your daddy doing?'

'He was lying on the floor with red stuff all around him,' she gulped.

'Did you know what the red stuff was, Nancy?'

She nodded.

'Blood. There was blood all over the floor.'

'And could you tell why your daddy was bleeding?'

Nancy nodded again.

'He looked like he was sleeping but I knew he wasn't because of all the red and the thing sticking out here.'

She gestured to her side.

'Nancy, I know this is so difficult but please can you explain what you mean by "the thing"? Can you tell me what was sticking out of him?'

'The knife,' she gulped. 'A big one from the block. The one that Mummy slices up the meat with on a Sunday.'

I had an overwhelming urge to go over and hug her but I knew I couldn't interfere.

She bravely described how she'd yelled for her mum but she couldn't find her, then she'd run out into the driveway and screamed for help.

'You're doing so well, Nancy,' Hayley told her. 'Would you like to have a break?'

Nancy shook her head. She turned round and looked at me at the back of the room and I gave her a reassuring smile.

'Nancy, I'd like to ask you a few things about your parents now, if that's OK?'

Hayley asked her about their families and if she had any grandparents, aunties, uncles or cousins.

'Daddy's parents died,' she said. 'And Mummy's are in France but I've never been there or seen them.'

'Did Mummy ever go and visit them?

Nancy shook her head.

'Daddy said they weren't very nice people so Mummy didn't want to see them any more.'

'And who were Mummy's friends?' Hayley asked her.

'I don't know,' she shrugged.

'Did Mummy have a best friend?'

'Oh, that was Daddy,' she smiled. 'He always said Mummy was his best friend. 'She didn't need any other friends. He always bought her lovely presents like sparkly jewellery and clothes and one time he even bought her a car.'

I knew she wanted to ask her about their relationship.

'And what about your mummy and daddy?' started Hayley. 'Did they ever get cross at each other or shout or get angry?'

Nancy didn't need time to think. She shook her head.

'No,' she said firmly. 'Never. They loved each other very much. Daddy looks after us,' she added. 'He loves us more than anything in the world. We have everything we've ever wanted and we are so lucky.'

It was sweet, but it struck me that it was an unusual thing for an eleven-year-old to say. The tone of Nancy's voice as she said it was almost robotic and I couldn't help but think from everything that she'd said about her parents, was how controlling Martin sounded.

After nearly an hour of questions, I could see Nancy was becoming weary. Juliet obviously felt the same way, so she asked Hayley if we could start wrapping things up.

'I think Nancy could do with a rest now,' she told her. 'But I'm sure she could come back another day if you wanted to ask her anything else.'

Hayley wrapped up the interview before she stood up and turned the cameras off.

'Thank you for talking to me and for being so brave, Nancy,' she smiled. 'You did really well.'

On the journey home, Nancy hardly said a word and I didn't push her to talk.

'I think I'm going to go to my room,' she told me when we got in.

'OK, flower,' I replied. 'You might want to have a little lie down. You look shattered.'

Half an hour later, I was just about to go and check on her when my phone rang. It was Juliet and I assumed she was ringing to see how Nancy was after this morning.

'Maggie?' she asked as I picked up.

I could tell by the tone of her voice that it wasn't a routine call.

'What is it?' I asked.

'Hayley just called,' she told me. 'They've found Helen.'

CHAPTER SIX

Lost and Found

Please don't let it be bad news, I willed to myself.

All I could think about was Nancy upstairs in her room and how she was going to cope if something had happened to her mum.

'Is she OK?' I asked.

'From what Hayley said, she seems to be fine,' Juliet told me, and my whole body sagged with relief.

She explained that Helen had been found at Dover just about to board a cross-Channel ferry to France. The police had put out an alert and one of the customs officials had recognised her from her photo.

Hayley was now on her way to Dover to collect her.

'She's going to bring her back to the police station to be questioned. 'She's tired but they don't think she needs medical treatment.'

I knew it was going to take hours before they were back.

'What do we do now then?' I asked. 'What do we tell Nancy?'

'We need to let her know what's happening,' replied Juliet. 'She deserves to know the truth. I'll come round now and talk to her.'

'OK,' I said.

Juliet hadn't yet gone back to her office after the police station. She was still doing home visits and was only twenty minutes away.

I went upstairs to see Nancy, who was lying on her bed reading. She looked up at me expectantly as I walked in.

'I just spoke to Juliet,' I told her. 'She's going to pop in.'

'Why?' she asked. 'We just saw her at the police station.'

'She just wants to check in and see how you're doing,' I told her.

Thankfully she seemed to accept it and didn't ask any more questions. While we waited, Nancy came downstairs and went out into the garden while I made myself a coffee. I sat on the patio, watching her play around on the swing. She seemed happy enough but when you looked closely, I could see the sadness in her eyes. I knew it was going to be such a relief for her to hear that her mum had been found, but who knew what was going to happen after that.

Suddenly there was a knock at the front door and Nancy ran into the house with me as I went to open it.

'What is it?' she asked Juliet. 'Have you come to tell me something?'

'Hold on lovey,' I smiled. 'At least let poor Juliet get in the door first.'

'Come through,' I told her, leading us all into the kitchen.

Nancy paced up and down the room and I could see that she was anxious.

'Come and sit down at the table with us,' I told her and begrudgingly she did.

'I wanted to let you know that DC Hirst phoned me half an hour ago to tell me that they've found your mum,' Juliet told her.

'Is she OK?' gasped Nancy, a worried look on her face. 'Where was she? Is she coming to get me now?'

'She's absolutely fine,' she told her. 'She's apparently a bit tired but other than that, we think she's OK.'

I could see the look of utter relief on Nancy's face.

'She was at Dover trying to get on a ferry to France,' she continued.

'Where is she now?' she asked. 'Can I see her? Is she at home? I can pack my things really quickly and go back home. It won't take me long, will it, Maggie?'

I glanced at Juliet.

'I'm afraid it's not as simple as that, Nancy,' she told her gently.

'At the moment your mum isn't going home. It's really important that the police talk to her. They want to ask her some questions about what happened the other night just like they did with you this morning.'

'Is she going to the police station too?' she asked.

'Yes, that's right,' nodded Juliet.

'But after that she can go home, can't she?' she asked. 'And I can go home too? 'I don't need to stay here if Mummy's back to look after me.'

I felt so sorry for Nancy.

'I know it's hard but we have to be patient and wait and see what happens,' I told her.

'Maggie's right,' nodded Juliet. 'Hayley's going to give me a ring from the police station and keep me updated. As soon as we know what's going on with your mum then we will let you know.'

Nancy nodded but I could see that she was close to tears.

'I just want to see my mummy,' she whimpered.

'I know you do,' Juliet soothed. 'Hayley knows that too so we'll try to make that happen as soon as we can, OK?'

I put my hand on hers and gave it a reassuring squeeze. She'd been through so much and I feared that there was so much more to come. She was such a sweet girl and this was just so shocking for any child to have to go through. To lose one parent in such a tragic way and then not to be able to see the other one must be so difficult for her.

'Nancy, do you want to go and watch some TV while I have a quick chat to Juliet?' I asked her.

'OK,' she nodded numbly.

She looked really downcast as she went off to the front room.

'So, what will happen with Helen now?' I asked, once Nancy had gone.

'Well, she's been arrested and the police have got twenty-four hours to question and charge her,' Juliet told me, 'but that can be extended if they need more time if it's something as serious as murder.'

'So it might not be until tomorrow that we hear anything?' I sighed.

'Possibly,' nodded Juliet.

We were going to have to play the waiting game and hope that Helen held the answers to what had happened in that house.

My main job for the rest of the day was to try to keep Nancy occupied, to keep her mind off things as best I could. I gave Louisa a quick ring.

'Do you fancy meeting us for a walk in the park?' I asked her.

Seeing Edie the other day had really cheered Nancy up and I hoped it would do the same thing again.

'Yes, that would be lovely,' she replied. 'We'd love to see you. I've deliberately been keeping away because I know Nancy's going through a hard time.'

'I think we could both do with the distraction today,' I explained.

Thankfully, Nancy seemed delighted to be seeing Louisa and Edie again. We had coffee and cake at the park café and Louisa let Nancy push the pram. There was no heavy conversation and for a couple of hours, Nancy seemed like a normal eleven-year-old girl, pulling faces at Edie and giggling.

I hadn't expected to hear anything more from Juliet that day but just after dinner, my mobile rang. Nancy was upstairs in her room and I was clearing away the dishes.

'Hayley just called me,' she said. 'I'm afraid they've charged Helen with murder.'

I almost dropped the phone.

'Oh no,' I sighed. 'Poor Nancy.'

Juliet described how she had confessed while she was being interviewed.

'Did she say why?' I asked.

'No,' replied Juliet. 'Hayley said she told them straight that she had done it but she refused to answer any other questions apparently.'

She'd calmly described how she'd got the knife from the block and stabbed Martin and then fled the scene. She was due to appear at the magistrate's court in the morning.

'What on earth do we tell Nancy?' I sighed.

'The truth,' replied Juliet.

I knew she was right. We owed it her to be honest and it was better coming from us rather than risk her hearing it from someone else or reading about it in a newspaper. It was important that she felt like she could trust us and it would be much more damaging if she heard it second-hand.

'I know it's late in the day, but I'll come round now if that's OK with you, Maggie,' Juliet told me. 'I don't want to leave this until the morning.'

Wanting to see her mother had been preying on Nancy's mind all day and Helen's arrest wasn't going to be an easy thing to tell her but she needed to know.

This time, I didn't tell Nancy that Juliet was coming. She was settled in her room and I didn't want her to panic or get anxious like she had done earlier. She was an intelligent girl and she would know instantly if something was wrong if her social worker was coming round for the second time that day.

When Juliet arrived half an hour later, I called her downstairs. When Nancy saw she was here again, her face fell.

'What is it?' she asked as I ushered us all into the living room and we sat down on the sofa. 'What's happened?'

Juliet took a deep breath and I reached for Nancy's hand.

'Your mum has spoken to the police and she's told them that she was the one who hurt your dad.'

Nancy blinked as she struggled to take it in.

'What do you mean?' she asked.

'Your mum has admitted to the police that she was the one who stabbed your dad with the knife,' she told her. 'I'm sorry, Nancy. I know this must be a terrible shock for you but we felt like you needed to know and we wanted to be honest with you.'

Nancy didn't say anything at first and then she started to shake her head frantically.

'No!' she shouted. 'The police have got it wrong. Mummy would never do that. She wouldn't hurt Daddy, she loved him. The police are lying.'

'I know it must be so hard for you to take in, but this is what Mummy has told the police,' Juliet explained.

'No,' she shouted. 'I don't believe you. Can I talk to them? I can tell them it wasn't Mummy and she's lying. It must have been a bad person who broke in, like I said, and did that to Daddy. The bad person must have scared Mummy and she ran away . . .'

Her voice trailed off as the tears came.

I gave her a hug.

'I know this must be so hard to understand,' I told her. 'I don't think any of us quite understand it yet. But we're here to answer any of your questions and we'll know more tomorrow.'

She sobbed in my arms, her whole body shaking.

'What will happen to her?' she whispered.

'She will have to stay at the police station tonight and in the morning she'll go to court,' Juliet told her.

'Then can she come home?' she asked.

'I'm afraid I don't know what's going to happen after that,' she replied.

'It's not fair,' whimpered Nancy.

She got up from the sofa and ran off upstairs. We heard her bedroom door slam.

Juliet and I looked at each other.

'We had to tell her the truth,' I sighed. 'It's going to take a while for it to sink in.'

'We did the right thing,' nodded Juliet.

She had to get back to the office but she agreed to let me know if there were any further updates.

'We probably won't know anything more until after court in the morning,' she told me. 'But we'll try to sort a visit out as soon as we can.'

I knew it would help Nancy if she could see her mum and talk to her face to face.

After Juliet had gone, I went upstairs to check on Nancy. To my surprise, Nancy was sitting at her desk drawing.

'What are you drawing?' I asked her.

'I'm making a card for Mummy,' she told me.

I looked at what she had drawn. There was a rainbow on the front and inside she'd written in the neatest handwriting:

I love you very much. I can't wait to see you and go back and live at our house together. I know you didn't hurt Daddy.

It was lovely but I knew I couldn't give her false hope.

As she carried on drawing, I talked to her.

'If what Mummy says is true and she did hurt your daddy, then I don't think she's going to be able to come home and live with you for quite a long time,' I told her gently. 'When somebody is accused of killing another person, then the judge will probably say your mum has to stay in prison until there's a court case. That's when a judge or a group of people called a jury decides if what your mum is saying is true.'

Nancy put her pen down and wouldn't turn around and look at me.

'I know I'm not supposed to be rude to adults, but I don't like what you're saying so I'm not listening to you any more.'

She put the pen down and got up and went to lie down on her bed.

I felt awful, but I couldn't let Nancy have false hope that her mum would be back at home soon. All the signs were that that wasn't going to happen but I knew it was so, so hard for her to understand. We had to be honest with her now because we couldn't hide the truth from her forever. She could see it on TV or read it in the newspaper or hear it from one of her friends when she eventually went back to school. I couldn't protect her from everything and I would rather she heard it from me.

I went downstairs and did a bit of tidying to give her a bit of space. When I went back up to see her, she'd got into her pyjamas and was ready for bed.

'I don't want to talk to you,' she told me, looking away.

'I'm sorry if what I said upset you, flower, and it's okay if you're angry with me, but I think it's important that we're honest with each other,' I replied. 'I didn't want you to get your hopes up and think that your mum was going to come home tomorrow. But what I do know is that Hayley and Juliet are going to try to arrange for you to see her as soon as they can and then you can talk to her yourself, okay?'

Nancy nodded.

'I want to go to bed now,' she said.

'Okay,' I smiled. 'Night night, flower. I'm really tired too so I think I'm going to go to bed as well. Remember I'm just down the landing so just come and get me or shout if you need me, OK?'

She nodded then lay down, turned away from me and curled up tight in a ball.

The first few nights with me she'd been so exhausted that she'd slept but tonight she was really unsettled.

At 1 a.m. I woke with a start to hear a tapping on my bedroom door.

'Maggie,' whispered a voice. 'I can't sleep. I lie down and close my eyes but nothing happens.'

I got Nancy to go back to bed and I went downstairs to make her some warm milk to try to help relax her.

I brought it up to her and sat by her bed on the floor.

'Would you like me to read to you?' I asked her and she nodded.

I grabbed one of the books that I'd put on her bedside table when she'd first arrived. It was an old Mallory Towers book by Enid Blyton.

As I started to read, she finished off her drink and then lay back down again. I could see her eyes fluttering and by the time I'd finished the first chapter, she was fast asleep.

'Night night, lovey,' I whispered. 'I hope tomorrow's a better day.'

The next morning, I tried to keep everything as normal as possible for Nancy. I avoided pushing her to talk about what had happened last night, but I couldn't get the thought of Helen out of my mind. I knew that she was due in court and I was waiting to hear the outcome. It was DC Hirst who called me just before lunchtime.

'Juliet said it was best to update you directly,' she told me. 'I wanted to let you know that Helen was formally charged with murder at the magistrates' court this morning.'

The case had been transferred to the Crown Court and as it was such a serious offence, she'd been remanded in custody.

There was no denying it now. Nancy had to accept that this was really happening and her mum was going to be in prison for the foreseeable future. Her world had been well and truly shattered.

CHAPTER SEVEN

The Truth Will Out

I listened as Hayley explained how Helen had been remanded in custody and was now on her way to a women's prison a couple of hours away.

'Did she plead guilty?' I asked.

'She hasn't had to submit a plea yet but she will do at her next court hearing, which will probably be in a few weeks' time,' she told me. 'We'll know then whether there's likely to be a trial or not.'

It was going to be a long and rocky road ahead of us.

'How's Nancy taken it?' she asked me.

'I think she's still in shock,' I told her. 'She refuses to believe that her mum would hurt her dad.'

'I can imagine,' sighed Hayley. 'When we were interviewing Helen, she admitted that she'd stabbed Martin but she refused point-blank to answer any of our questions about why she'd done it.

'She was strangely calm and very matter-of-fact about it – it was all very odd. I'm hoping that further down the line when she's spoken to her solicitor, things will be a bit clearer.'

'Do you think it could have been self-defence?' I asked hopefully.

Hayley explained that Helen had been checked over by a police doctor after her arrest but she didn't have any bruises or injuries that suggested there had been a scuffle or a fight.

'The autopsy report said the same about Martin's body,' she told me. 'No bruises or scratches, just a single stab wound.'

We were all desperately searching for answers.

'Do you think Nancy would like to see her mum?' Hayley asked.

'Yes, definitely,' I said at once. 'She keeps asking about it and I think it would be a really good idea.'

'I'll get on to the prison now and try to get something arranged and let Juliet know. It's probably going to take a few days to arrange.'

'Thanks,' I told her. 'I'd really appreciate that.'

'Oh, and Maggie, I should warn you that it might be on the news today about Helen,' she added. 'There were a couple of reporters at court.'

'Thanks for the heads-up,' I said.

I would definitely make sure that I kept the radio off and make sure Nancy didn't watch any TV today.

When Juliet called half an hour later, I was worried it was more bad news. I told her that I'd spoken to Hayley and we were waiting to hear from her about a prison visit.

'While we wait to hear about that, I wanted to talk to you about school,' she told me. 'I don't know how you feel, but I think it would do Nancy good to go back to school next week.'

'It will be hard for her but I think it's probably a good idea,' I agreed.

School was the only familiar thing left in Nancy's life and she could do with some stability and routine. It would be good for her to see her friends and have some structure in her day.

Juliet explained she'd spoken to her head teacher, Michelle Judd, on the phone and she was keen to come round and see Nancy.

'She asked if she could possibly pop round today,' she told me. 'Would that work? She seems very nice and they're all very concerned about Nancy.'

I was about to say that I didn't think it was a good idea as, after a restless night's sleep, I could see Nancy was absolutely shattered. But then I remembered how happy she'd been to see Louisa and Edie and I thought perhaps she could do with another distraction to try to take her mind off things. Plus it would be nice for her to see a familiar face.

'OK,' I said. 'We're just going to have a quiet day at home so tell her to pop round any time.'

When I got off the phone with Juliet, I broached the subject with Nancy.

'Miss Judd is going to come round to see you today,' I told her.

'Why?' she asked suspiciously.

'She wants to see you and also wants to talk to you about possibly going back to school next week.'

'Next week?' she asked.

I could see her mulling it over in her mind.

'Yes, sweetie. We thought you might be missing your friends and it would be good for you to go back and see them.'

'I do want to see my friends,' she sighed. 'But what if people stare at me or ask me questions and stuff? I don't want to talk about it.'

'Well, that's something we can discuss with Miss Judd,' I told her and she nodded.

She arrived just before lunch. Micheline Judd was an impeccably dressed woman in her fifties. She was very well spoken and seemed genuinely compassionate and caring. Nancy was very polite to her and I could tell that she liked her.

'Hello, Miss Judd,' she said. 'Thank you for coming to visit me.'

The head teacher put an arm on her shoulder.

'We were so very sorry to hear about your father, Nancy,' she told her. 'Everyone at school is thinking of you.'

'Thank you,' she said, looking down at the floor at the mention of her dad.

'I've been talking to your social worker, and we thought it would be good for you to come back to school next week,' she continued. 'I know your friends are missing you and your teachers will be very pleased to see you.'

'But I don't want to go back if everyone's talking about me and asking questions about my dad,' she sighed. 'It would make me too sad.'

'If you don't want to talk about it then that's absolutely fine,' Miss Judd reassured her. 'I'll make sure that everyone is aware.'

I made us all a drink and Miss Judd chatted about what had been going on at school and how the end of term production was coming up soon.

'I also wanted to bring you this,' she told her, handing her a copy of *Charlotte's Web*. 'It's what your form is reading at the moment. There's absolutely no pressure but I know how much you love books and what a good reader you are so I wanted you to have it.'

'Thank you, Miss Judd,' Nancy replied politely.

I was keen to have a quick chat to Miss Judd privately.

'Nancy, do you think you've got all the uniform that you need for next week?' I asked her. 'I know Juliet picked up a few things from your house but I'm not sure if she managed to get everything.'

'I don't know,' she shrugged.

'Well why don't you run upstairs and check?'

'If there's anything missing then I can make sure we have it ready for you at school first thing on Monday,' Miss Judd told her kindly.

When Nancy went upstairs, she turned to me. 'It's such a terrible business,' she sighed. 'I can hardly believe what's happened. How's Nancy doing?'

I explained how she was very up and down and quite tearful.

'The poor child,' she sighed. 'Everyone at school is struggling to understand it. They seemed like such a nice family. As I was telling the social worker, her fees are always paid in advance in a lump sum – in fact I talked to our bursar and Mr Miller has paid until next year. He's always very generous when it comes to fundraising campaigns and raffle prizes. We're all just so shocked. Helen seems like a lovely woman too.'

'It's a very difficult situation,' I nodded. 'I think everyone who knew the family is in shock.'

A few minutes later, Nancy came back down and our conversation abruptly ended.

'It's just my PE kit,' she told us. 'I haven't got that.'

'I will make sure that we have one all ready for you at school so don't you worry,' Miss Judd told her.

She only stayed for half an hour but Nancy seemed genuinely pleased to have seen her.

'I think it's a good idea to go back to school next week,' she told me after Miss Judd had left. 'I think I'd like to. Daddy always likes me to work hard and do well at school.'

I gave her a sympathetic smile and squeezed her hand.

'I'm so proud of you,' I told her. 'I know it will be hard for you but I do think it will be good for you rather than being stuck here with me, which I know is really boring.'

She even gave me a little smile back.

The rest of the day was very quiet. Nancy started to read the book Miss Judd had given her and I caught up on paperwork. I also got a call from Becky from the fostering agency I worked for.

'How are things going with the new placement?' she asked.

I told her what had been going on.

'I've been chasing Juliet for paperwork for the fostering agreement,' she said. 'But I've not heard anything back from her.'

I explained that Helen had only just been found and arrested. Because she'd been missing, Helen hadn't signed any of the Social Services' forms to give permission for Nancy to go into the care system.

'Oh, that explains it,' Becky sighed.

Now that Helen was on her way to prison, Juliet could liaise with the prison social worker there.

'For all we know, there could be a relative or a friend who could take Nancy,' Becky told me.

'I'm expecting to hear from Juliet later about a possible prison visit to see Nancy's mum,' I told her. 'She will be going too so she can bring papers for Helen to sign then.'

In fostering, there was always a lot of admin when a new child arrived. The most important things for me were the delegated responsibility forms that gave me permission to seek medical treatment if Nancy was ill, take her to the GP, opticians or dentist, or get her hair cut.

'Well, keep me posted,' Becky told me, as she said goodbye.

It wasn't until the following day that Juliet had some news.

'We can take Nancy to see Helen at the prison tomorrow,' she told me. 'It's a specially arranged visit outside of normal visiting hours as a one-off.'

This was good news as it meant we wouldn't be in a busy room full of other prisoners and visitors, so it would be less intimidating for Nancy.

'Do you want me to come round and talk to Nancy about it?' she asked.

'It's okay,' I replied. 'I'll do it.'

I'd been into several prisons during the years I'd been fostering and although I hadn't been to this particular prison before, the procedures and processes were generally the same. I could talk Nancy through what would happen when we got there and answer any of her questions.

'I can drive us all there tomorrow if that would help?' asked Juliet.

'That would be great,' I replied.

If I didn't have to worry about the drive and finding my way, it meant I could concentrate fully on Nancy and make sure she was okay.

As soon as I got off the phone, I went to Nancy's bedroom to see her.

'So tomorrow we're going to go and see your mummy,' I told her.

Nancy's face lit up.

'Oh, is she home?' she gasped. 'I told you the police had got it all wrong.'

'I'm afraid not, flower,' I said. 'Remember what Juliet told you? The judge decided that your mum has to stay in prison so they have more time to talk to her and try to work out what happened to your dad.

'I know you want to see her, so the prison have arranged a special visit for you, me and Juliet.'

I could see the disappointment on her face as her hopes faded.

'I don't suppose you've ever been inside a prison before?'

Nancy shook her head.

'But I've seen one on TV,' she told me. 'Will Mummy be in handcuffs chained to some men?'

'No, I don't think she'll be in handcuffs,' I said. 'There'll be prison officers there but they'll just be walking around.'

Nancy was old enough to understand and we had to be honest with her about what the visit was going to be like. I explained what would probably happen when we went in. How we would have to sign in, then walk through a scanner and then we'd probably be searched by security guards.

'But why do they do that?' she asked.

'It's just to make sure we're not bringing anything into the prison that we shouldn't be,' I told her. 'Even though we know that we're not, they do have to check.'

I reassured her that Juliet and I would be with her every step of the way and answer any questions that she might have.

'Is there anything you want to know?' I asked her.

'What will the building be like?' she questioned. 'Does it have bars on the windows and that spiky metal stuff on top of the walls?

'I've visited people in prison before but I've never been to the one your mummy is in,' I told her. 'So we'll both have to wait and see what it looks like.'

'Does Mummy have her own room or does she have to share one? Will we all fit in it when we go and visit?'

I could see that at this point she was more intrigued than anything else.

'We won't be going into the place where your mum sleeps,' I told her. 'We'll go and meet her in a big visitors' room where there will be lots of chairs and tables. They've arranged for us to have a special visit so there won't be lots of other people there at the same time – just your mum and us. Is that OK?' I asked her and she nodded.

'Oh, I can take her the card that I made for her,' she smiled.

I hated destroying her hopes but I knew I had to be honest with her.

'I'm afraid we're not allowed to bring anything in to give to Mummy, flower,' I told her.

'But why not?' she asked, looking crushed.

The truth was you couldn't take in drawings, cards or pictures because some people soaked drugs into the paper or crushed them up into paints to smuggle them into prisons. Then inmates would eat them or smoke them. I didn't want to have to explain that to Nancy though.

77

'I'm sure we can leave it at reception though and they'll give it to your mum later on.'

I was sure the prison staff would be able to test it or photocopy it and then pass it on to Helen so Nancy's efforts weren't wasted.

For the rest of the afternoon, the questions came thick and fast and I did my best to answer them. But as the day turned to night, I could tell Nancy was getting nervous.

'It will be OK,' I told her as I tucked her in that night. 'Juliet and I will be with you and I know your mum is going to be so pleased to see you.'

To be honest, I felt equally apprehensive. As a foster carer, I don't look forward to taking a child into prison and it never gets any easier. It always makes me feel claustrophobic and on edge and I always worry about getting out if there's a fire. I knew that, emotionally, it was going to be really hard for Nancy. All I could think about as I drifted off to sleep that night was how on earth Nancy was going to react.

CHAPTER EIGHT

Behind Bars

Turning my head around, I looked at Nancy sitting in the back seat.

'How are you doing?' I asked her.

'OK,' she shrugged, but the expression on her face told me otherwise.

We were on our way to visit Helen in prison and I could see the fear and the worry in Nancy's eyes. I'd done my best to reassure her, but for any child, going to see a parent in prison is a scary prospect. I knew from visiting prisons myself in the past that even for an adult, it was a very unsettling and vulnerable experience. I was also very conscious that this would be the first time that Nancy had seen her mum since her dad had died and she had been charged with his murder; there must have been so many conflicting emotions running through her head.

'Not much longer now,' smiled Juliet from the driver's seat. 'The satnav's showing that we're nearly there.'

We'd been in the car for nearly two hours. It'd had been an early start and Nancy already looked exhausted.

Fifteen minutes later, on the outskirts of a large town, we followed the signs that directed us into a side road. I could see Nancy anxiously looking out of the window.

'Here we are,' said Juliet as we drove towards a barrier with a booth to the side of it.

The prison was a large, modern two-storey building with a high wall running around the outside of it.

'Oh, it looks a bit like a secondary school,' said Nancy, who sounded surprised.

'Yes I know what you mean, lovey,' I said, trying to keep my voice light.

It was a huge sprawling site in the middle of open land. As we drove towards the barrier, Juliet wound down her window and told the security guard why we were there. He checked our names off a list and pointed us towards the visitor's car park.

As it wasn't an official visiting day, there was plenty of space.

'Right then,' smiled Juliet, opening up the passenger door for Nancy. 'Our visit isn't for half an hour but we have to go and register at the visitor's centre first.'

It was a separate building in the prison grounds close to the car park. A female security guard checked our names off another list and Juliet and I showed her our ID.

'I'm sorry, but with it not being an official visiting time, our kiosk isn't open today,' she told us. 'But I can ask one of my colleagues to sort you out with a drink if you'd like one?'

'I'd love a cup of tea with milk,' Juliet told her. 'And you, Maggie?'

'Yes, please,' I nodded.

It had been an early start and a long drive and I was parched.

'Nancy, would you like anything?' I asked her but she shook her head.

I could see she was really nervous. We sat down on the plastic chairs that were attached to the floor in rows. As well as the drinks kiosk, there was a little playroom where children could go while they waited, and some toilets.

'Nancy, now would be a good time for you to go to the loo,' Juliet told her. 'It might be your only chance before you go and see your mummy.'

'OK,' she sighed.

'Do you want me to come with you?' I asked, but she shook her head.

I was glad she'd gone as normally if you needed to go to the toilet during a visit, a prison officer would have to go with you and search you beforehand and afterwards. I didn't want to have to put her through that. I didn't want to go through it myself either so I was going to go when Nancy came back.

'Poor girl,' I sighed. 'I can see she's a bundle of nerves.'

'I'm not surprised,' nodded Juliet. 'Prisons are not nice places for anyone to visit.'

Neither of us were sure how she was going to react when she saw her mum either.

Prison visits always involve a lot of waiting around and it was close to an hour before one of the security guards directed us towards the main building.

'They'll take you through security over there,' she told us.

As we walked across the car park towards the main entrance, I felt Nancy's hand reach out for mine and I gave it a reassuring squeeze.

'It's going to be OK, flower,' I told her. 'We're right here with you.'

The main prison reception was huge and echoey. You weren't allowed to take any of your personal belongings into the visiting hall with you so first of all we had to put all our bags and coats into a locker. Then we had to go through security.

'Remember I told you about these?' I told Nancy. 'These arches are metal detectors and we have to walk through them one by one.'

'I'll go first so you can see how easy it is,' Juliet told her.

'Oh, it's a bit like at the airport when you go on holiday,' Nancy whispered to me.

'Yes, you're right,' I smiled.

We waited while Juliet walked through and then it was Nancy's turn.

'You go now, lovey,' I told her.

'Come on darling,' the female prison officer told her, sensing her hesitation.

Thankfully we all managed to walk through them without any alarms going off.

'Now I'm going to give you a pat-down search,' the prison officer explained.

'What's that?' asked Nancy nervously.

'Remember we talked about how someone would pat us all down our arms and legs, just to check we're not bringing anything into the prison?' I told her.

'But I'm not,' she said.

'We know that, but they need to check,' I told her. 'I'll go first.'

As she was a social worker, Juliet didn't need to be searched. It was always a bit of a snub for me that lawyers and social workers were deemed as professionals and were normally exempt from searches when they attended prison in a work capacity but foster carers weren't.

'See,' I smiled as the prison officer patted me down. 'It only takes a few seconds.'

But Nancy didn't look convinced. Even more so when a burly security guard appeared with a German shepherd that I guessed was a drugs detection dog.

'This is Effie,' he told us. 'She's just going to have a little sniff around you.'

Nancy looked terrified and as the dog came towards us, I felt her press herself against me.

'It's OK,' I told her. 'They won't let her off the lead and she's not going to hurt you.'

Prison dogs were trained to detect the scent of drugs on visitors. Even if they picked up something, they wouldn't bark, they'd just sit quietly next to the person.

'I'll take you through to the visit room now,' the female prison officer told us and I think Nancy was relieved to get out of there.

I took hold of her hand again as the officer led us through a series of air-locked doors. Even though I'd been into prisons many times, I always felt my chest tightening and a slight sense of panic rising up in me as we went through one locked door after another.

Nancy looked around with wide eyes as we walked down the bare corridors. None of them had any windows so they were harshly lit but they had glass panels running across the top which let light in from other areas of the prison.

'It looks a bit dirty and scruffy here,' she sighed. 'Mummy won't like it.'

As we walked down one corridor, the sound of somebody screaming and swearing in another part of the building echoed around the tiled walls. I could see the fear in Nancy's eyes.

'It's okay, flower,' I reassured her. 'We're nearly there now.'

The visiting hall was a large room filled with chairs and tables all set out in little groups. I was glad we were the only ones there today as I could imagine the noise was overwhelming when the whole place was full of people. The furniture was all secured to the floor and each little group consisted of three blue plastic seats joined together in a row, a low table in the middle and a black plastic chair facing them.

The prison officer led us over to a group of seats at the far end of the room.

'You can sit down here,' she said.

'Where's Mummy?' asked Nancy, looking around worriedly. 'Why isn't she here?'

'She'll be brought through shortly,' the officer told her. 'We like to bring the visitors in first.'

The three of us sat down on a row of blue plastic seats.

'When Mummy comes in, she'll sit there,' I told her, pointing to the black seat facing us.

Then there was more waiting. Nancy fidgeted nervously in her seat as I looked around the room.

There was another kiosk for drinks and snacks that was closed and in the corner was a small sectioned-off area with a worn plastic playhouse and mini slide in it and a few baskets of grubby-looking toys.

I couldn't help but think how difficult it must be for younger children to have to come and see a parent in prison. Prisoners had to stay seated during their visit and couldn't walk around so if their child wanted to go off and play in the play area, they couldn't go with them. I'd had a couple of situations like that and it was really hard and frustrating for the parent. At least Nancy was older and had more of an understanding about what was happening.

'When is she coming?' asked Nancy, staring anxiously at the door. 'It's been ages.'

'She'll be here soon, don't worry,' Juliet reassured her.

But it was another ten long minutes before the door finally opened.

A tall female prison officer walked into the visit room followed by a figure shuffling in behind her. Helen was petite with long straight brown hair like Nancy's and the same big brown eyes. She was a very pretty woman but she looked pale and washed out and there were purple shadows under her eyes. The baggy grey tracksuit that she was wearing hung off her slender body.

'Oh it's Mummy,' gasped Nancy.

But she didn't get up off her chair or run over and try to hug her, she hung back, looking unsure of what to do.

'You can sit down, Helen,' the prison officer instructed her and she did what he said.

Helen looked like she was in a daze as she shuffled over to the black plastic chair. There was a strange vague look in her eyes; it was almost as if she was in a trance.

'Hello, Helen,' said Juliet. 'I'm Nancy's social worker and this is Maggie. She's the foster carer who Nancy's currently staying with.'

'Oh,' she nodded.

She seemed very vague and not with it. Nancy just sat there, staring at her.

'Mummy, it doesn't look like you,' she said. 'Where are your lovely clothes?'

Helen looked down at herself almost as if she hadn't noticed what she was wearing.

'I didn't have anything with me, darling,' she told her, in a soft French accent. 'So they gave me this.'

I noticed the prison officer who had brought Helen in was sitting at a nearby table.

'Why is that lady watching us?' asked Nancy.

'She's a prison officer,' Juliet told her. 'It's her job to supervise the visits and make sure everyone is sticking to the rules.'

'I don't like it here,' Nancy said firmly. 'I want you to come home, Mummy.'

Helen didn't say anything, she just stared down at the floor.

Nancy hadn't given her a hug yet but I didn't want to push her if she didn't want to. She looked like she was struggling to know what to say to her mother and an awkward silence hung in the air.

Juliet and I gave each other a look – as if we both recognised that one of us had to step in here.

'Are they looking after you, okay?' Juliet asked Helen. 'Is the food all right?'

'I don't know,' sighed Helen. 'I haven't been eating anything. I'm not really hungry . . .'

Her voice trailed off.

'Don't worry, Mummy,' Nancy told her cheerfully. 'When the police find out they've made a mistake, we can go home to our house can't we?'

Helen didn't say anything. She looked down at her hands and I could see that they were shaking.

Suddenly, totally out of the blue, Nancy burst into tears.

'I'm so sad about Daddy,' she sobbed. 'I miss him.'

She got up off her chair and threw her arms around Helen's neck. Helen held her while she cried and she curled up on her lap like a baby.

'I miss him too darling,' she whispered, burying her head in Nancy's hair. I could see she was crying too.

Tears pricked my own eyes. I could feel Helen and Nancy's pain and it felt like Juliet and I were almost intruding as we witnessed this tender moment between mother and daughter.

A few minutes later, the prison officer came over to us.

'Could I ask you please to sit back on your chair,' she told Nancy gently. 'I'm sorry but it's the rules. Physical contact is only allowed at the beginning and the end of a visit.'

'Come and sit back down, sweetie,' Juliet told her.

I was surprised, as when it came to children's visits, I'd never known physical contact to be limited in that way. I was sure that prison officers didn't have to be that strict but it wasn't really the time or the place to argue against it. In the past, I'd taken children to visit their parents in prison and they'd had as much physical contact as they wanted. However, I remembered these children had been little ones aged under five, so a lot younger than Nancy.

I thought it was a bit harsh to enforce rules like that with any child, but Nancy did what she was told and went back to her seat. I passed her a tissue to dry her face and gave her a sympathetic smile.

I could tell so many thoughts were running through her head and suddenly, out of the blue, she asked Helen a question.

'Mummy, why are the police lying and saying that you hurt Daddy?'

My heart started thumping. I looked at Juliet anxiously.

Helen stared at the floor and didn't make eye contact with her.

'Why are they lying, Mummy?' Nancy asked again. 'Why don't you tell them it's not true, then we can go home and live in our house again?'

Helen put her head in her hands and I could see her entire body was shaking.

'I can't,' she sobbed. 'I can't do that.'

'Mummy, why won't you tell them,' begged Nancy. 'Please just tell them that you didn't hurt Daddy.'

'I can't, darling,' gulped Helen. 'I can't because I did.'

She looked up, her bloodshot brown eyes staring straight at her daughter.

'I did it, Nancy. The police aren't lying – I was the one who hurt Daddy. I stuck the knife in him.'

She started to cry quietly. Nancy looked utterly stunned as if someone had slapped her in the face.

'How could you do that?' she shouted. 'How could you hurt my daddy? I loved him.'

'I'm sorry, darling,' sobbed Helen. 'I'm so sorry.'

Nancy stood up.

'I hate you,' she yelled. 'I hate you for killing my daddy and taking him away from us. I never want to see you or talk to you again.'

'Please, Nancy,' Helen begged. 'Please forgive me.'

She got up and tried to put her arms around Nancy but Nancy pushed her away.

'Get off me,' she yelled. 'I don't love you any more.'

She got up off her chair and stormed off.

Helen stood up, tears streaming down her face.

'Nancy, please,' she wept. 'Come back.'

The prison officer came rushing over to us.

'Can you sit down,' she told Helen firmly. 'Otherwise this visit will be over and I'll have to take you back to your cell.'

To a large extent, it felt like the visit was already over. Nancy had stormed off but she couldn't go anywhere as the doors to the visit room were locked. So she stood in the corner, slumped against the wall with her back to us.

'I'm just going to check to see if she's OK,' I told Juliet.

As soon as I walked over to her, I could tell she was crying.

'I want to go,' she told me tearfully. 'Please, Maggie, can you take me back outside?'

'I know you're upset, lovey, but let's sit down and talk for a few minutes,' I told her. I knew that once we left, we wouldn't be allowed back in.

We sat down on some chairs near to the door and I put my arm around her.

'I know this is all really hard and upsetting for you and it's all very confusing but I don't know when you're going to be able to see your mum next,' I told her. 'And I don't want you to leave her when you're feeling sad and upset like this. And your mummy is very sad and upset too.'

'Good,' she spat. 'I hate her for what she's done.'

'I know you're feeling angry and confused but why don't you at least go and say goodbye to her?'

Nancy shook her head firmly.

'I want to go,' she told me. 'Please, Maggie.'

She had a right to decide what she wanted to do and I could see there was no persuading her. I went back over to Juliet, who was comforting Helen.

'Nancy's very upset and she says she wants to go,' I told her.

Just then another prison officer came in.

'I can take you both to reception and you can wait there,' he said.

'I'll stay here for now,' Juliet told me. 'I need a few minutes with Helen and to get her to sign some forms. I'll see you outside.'

'OK,' I nodded.

As the prison officer opened up the door so we could leave the visit room, I gave Nancy one last chance to change her mind.

'Are you sure you don't want to go back and say goodbye to Mummy?'

'No,' she said firmly. 'She killed my daddy. I never want to see her again.'

With that, the prison officer opened the door and Nancy stormed out.

CHAPTER NINE

School Days

Nancy and I sat in silence in the prison reception, waiting for Juliet. I could tell her anger had quickly turned to upset and she looked totally and utterly devastated.

Her entire world had just fallen apart. She'd obviously convinced herself that the police had got it wrong, that her mum hadn't killed her dad. But now Helen had admitted it to her and I couldn't even imagine how distressed she must be.

'Gosh that must have been so hard for you seeing your mum and hearing what she had to say,' I told her gently. 'You must feel really confused about everything.'

'I don't want to talk about it,' she mumbled, not making eye contact with me.

'Well you know that I'm here for you if you do,' I replied.

I didn't want to push her to talk as I could see how draining the visit had been for her. I knew I just needed to get her out of the prison.

Eventually, twenty minutes later, Juliet came out.

'Are you OK, Nancy?' she asked her. 'Your mum's very upset about the way the visit ended and she wanted me to tell you that she's sorry that she didn't say goodbye to you.'

'I don't care,' sighed Nancy. 'She killed my daddy and I don't ever want to see her again.'

I knew we all needed to get out of the oppressive atmosphere of the prison and I felt my shoulders sag with relief as we left the building and walked outside into the fresh air. I could see Nancy was totally wiped out.

'I think I'm going to sit in the back with her,' I told Juliet quietly as we walked towards the car.

I thought Nancy might ask why I wasn't getting in the front but she didn't say a word. As we set off, she rested her head on my shoulder and closed her eyes.

Ten minutes later, I could see that she was in a deep sleep.

'She's absolutely spark out,' I told Juliet.

'Poor girl,' she sighed. 'That was so hard for her. I really felt for both of them. Helen was completely distraught after Nancy left.'

'Did she say anything else or give you any indication why she might have done what she did?' I asked.

'Nothing,' shrugged Juliet. 'I think she's still in shock about what's happened and she hasn't been sleeping or eating. She just seemed very vague and not quite with it.'

I also knew it was neither mine nor Juliet's job to ask Helen those sorts of probing questions. That was down to the police and her solicitor. Our concern was always going to be Nancy.

'I think that's what Nancy's going to struggle with,' I replied. 'It's enough to try to cope with the fact that your mum killed your dad but to not even know or understand why must make it even harder.'

Meeting Helen had left me even more puzzled as she had come across as such a nice, gentle woman. At this moment in time, none of us had a clue about what had gone on in that house.

Nancy slept the entire way back. She didn't even wake up as Juliet pulled up outside my house.

'Bless her,' I sighed. 'She obviously really needed this.'

'What are your plans for the next few days?' Juliet asked me.

'Not much at all,' I replied.

I already knew we were going to have a very quiet rest of the day as Nancy was exhausted. I explained that I was going to spend the weekend making sure that she was ready for school on Monday.

'How's she feeling about school?' asked Juliet.

'I can see she's really nervous about going back but she says she wants to go,' I told her.

Gently, I woke Nancy up. She was still very groggy as I led her into the house.

'Come on, let's get you some lunch,' I told her.

'I'm not hungry,' she sighed.

She spent the rest of the afternoon in her bedroom. I checked on her from time to time but I could tell that she just wanted to be left alone with her thoughts and I had to respect that. I did want her to eat something though so later that afternoon, I took her up a sandwich. Nancy was curled up on her bed.

'I brought you some food,' I told her gently. 'You must be starving.'

'Thank you but I don't want anything,' she murmured.

No matter what she was feeling, she was always so polite.

I put the plate on her bedside table and knelt down on the floor next to her bed.

'It must have been so difficult seeing your mum today and hearing what she said to you,' I told her gently. 'How do you feel about it?'

'Please don't ask me,' she begged. 'I can't talk about it.'

I could see how raw it was for her and I understood. You can't push children to open up to you. She needed time and space and hopefully she would talk to me when she was ready.

The weekend was quiet. I could see Nancy was still exhausted and was happy so stay in the house so I didn't push her to do anything. Becky phoned to check how things were going and Louisa rang too.

'I thought I might pop round with Edie,' she told me.

'You know I'd normally love that,' I told her. 'And you know how much Nancy loves seeing Edie but I just don't think it's a good idea at the moment.'

I explained that we'd been to the prison to see Helen.

'Poor thing,' she sighed. 'I heard it on the news about her mum being charged with murder. It's awful.'

'It really is,' I told her. 'And it's a lot for an eleven-year-old to get her head around.'

'Don't worry if you can't tell me, but do you know why her mum did it?' asked Louisa.

'Not a clue,' I sighed. 'That's what's so hard for Nancy.'

'Well, tell her I'm thinking of her,' Louisa told me. 'She's such a sweet girl.'

I knew Nancy had enough on her mind so I didn't mention school until Sunday morning.

'It will be so nice for you to see your friends again,' I smiled. 'This afternoon we'll get all your uniform laid out and make sure everything is ready.'

I could tell by the look on her face that she was worried about it.

'How am I going to get there?' she asked. 'Mummy always drives me to school.'

'Don't worry, I can take you, flower,' I told her. 'And Miss Judd said you can start a bit later than normal tomorrow and she will come and meet us and take you to your classroom.'

When I'd looked up where her school was, I realised that it was quite a drive from my house. To get her there for 8.20 a.m. we'd have to leave around 7.30, so the delayed start tomorrow was very welcome. They were long school days though and I wouldn't need to collect her until 4.30 p.m. every afternoon.

At bedtime, I could see Nancy was getting really anxious.

'Does everyone know what's happened to my parents?' she asked me. 'What if they're all staring at me or asking me questions?'

'Miss Judd will have spoken to the other pupils and told them that you don't want to talk about it,' I told her. 'But if anybody's saying anything that upsets you then you tell Miss Judd or your tutor, OK?'

She nodded but she still looked terrified.

'It will be fine,' I reassured her. 'I bet it will feel really nice being back in school and being with your friends again. And surely anything must be better than hanging round with me all day?' I joked and she gave me a weak smile.

*

'What a lovely place,' I gasped, as I drove through a huge iron gate and pulled into the car park.

Nancy's school was a grand Victorian building with a modern extension to the side of it. It was surrounded by rolling grounds and in the distance, I could see tennis courts and all sorts of sports pitches.

'Shall we go in then?' I smiled, taking my seatbelt off. 'Miss Judd will be waiting for us.'

'I-I-can't,' stuttered Nancy, her face suddenly draining of colour. 'I feel funny. I'm really hot and I can't breathe.'

I quickly wound down the window on her side of the car to let some fresh air in.

'Take a deep breath, hold it in for a few seconds and then blow it out through your mouth,' I told her, showing her what to do.

She took a few shallow, gulping breaths.

'It's not working,' she gasped. 'I don't feel well, Maggie.'

I could see that she was panicking.

'You're okay, lovey,' I soothed. 'Keep taking those big, deep breaths.'

I passed her a bottle of water and encouraged her to take little sips to help cool her down. Thankfully after ten minutes or so, I could see that she was starting to get calmer and her breathing was slowing down.

'See, you're OK,' I smiled. 'Your body can do strange things when you're feeling worried. School will be fine and if it's not or it gets too much then tell Miss Judd and she'll phone me and I'll come and get you, OK?'

She nodded bravely. I wouldn't normally give kids a get-out clause with school but I felt that after everything she'd been through recently, Nancy needed one. My heart went out to her. It was hard enough facing people after a bereavement but even more so when your parent had been killed in such tragic circumstances and you and your family's business had been all over the media.

We got out of the car and we walked up the grand entrance steps into reception. Someone in the office called Miss Judd and she came straight out to meet us.

'Hi there, Nancy,' she smiled. 'I'm so pleased to see you and I know how much your friends are looking forward to having you back. Before we go to your classroom, shall we give Maggie a quick tour?'

'Okay miss,' she shrugged.

We walked through the corridors and Nancy pointed out the gym and the swimming pool, the drama studio and the music rooms. I could see it was a clever tactic from Miss Judd to take her mind off things and help get her more relaxed.

'And here we are at your classroom, Nancy,' she smiled.

'Bye lovey,' I told her. 'I'll see you tonight. I hope you have a great day.'

'Thank you,' she said meekly. I could see that anxious look on her face again.

Miss Judd pushed open the classroom door where rows of smartly dressed girls had their heads down doing their work.

Nancy looked back at me nervously.

'Go on,' I nodded. 'It will be OK.'

A couple of the girls looked up and waved excitedly when

they saw her standing there. Her teacher, a young blonde woman, walked over to us.

'Nancy, I'm so pleased that you're back,' she smiled. 'Come and take your seat. We're just reading *Jane Eyre*.'

Hesitantly, she walked into the classroom and I gave her a little wave before the door closed behind us.

'Don't you worry, she'll be absolutely fine,' Miss Judd told me. 'We'll keep a close eye on her.'

'Thank you,' I replied.

I knew having the familiarity and the routine of school would be good for Nancy, but part of me did wonder whether it was a little bit too soon after her dad's death and her mum's arrest. I guessed only time would tell.

I spent the whole day until pick up thinking and worrying about Nancy. I waited in the car park and, as she walked towards me, she couldn't wait to get in the car.

'I was going to try to have a quick word with Miss Judd,' I told her.

'Please can we just go?' she sighed. 'I'm so tired.'

'OK,' I said.

I could give Miss Judd a call tomorrow when she was back in school.

'How did your day go?' I asked her on the drive home. 'Was it nice to be with your friends? If there's anybody you'd like to invite back for dinner one evening then just let me know.'

'What, so they'll all know I'm in foster care?' she sighed.

I could see that she was really upset.

'We don't have to say anything – you can just say that you're staying with me for a bit,' I told her.

'It's not fair,' she mumbled and I could see she was close to tears. 'Everyone knows what's happened to me and my family.'

'I'm sorry, lovey,' I told her. 'I know it's hard for you but hopefully things will feel easier tomorrow now you've got the first day out of the way.'

The following day, I was convinced that she wasn't going to want to go to school. But, although she wasn't very chatty, Nancy got up and got dressed and into the car. She didn't say a word during the journey and I was expecting the worst when we got to school. But, much to my surprise, when I pulled up into the car park she got out and went in without any objection. It was as if she had resigned herself to the fact that she had to go in.

I had a morning of doing admin and was just about to call my boyfriend, Graham, for a long overdue catch-up when my mobile rang.

It was Nancy's school's number.

'Hi Maggie, it's Micheline Judd.'

I could tell by the urgency in her voice that something had happened.

'What is it?' I asked. 'Do I need to come and pick Nancy up?'

'I'm afraid she's gone,' she told me.

'Gone?' I gasped. 'What on earth do you mean?'

She explained that at afternoon registration twenty minutes ago, Nancy's teacher had realised that she wasn't there.

'Somehow she must have left at lunchtime,' she told me.

Staff had searched the school building and the grounds but there was no sign of her, and her friends hadn't seen her in the cafeteria at lunchtime.

'But how did she get out?' I asked, remembering the buzzer on the doors at reception that you had to press so that someone could let you in and out.

'Well, she didn't come out through the front entrance but I suppose if someone really wanted to get out and they were quite small and nimble, there are ways to climb over the wall at the back of the grounds.'

A panicky feeling started to rise up in my chest.

'Have you called the police?' I asked her.

'Not yet,' she said. "I wanted to speak to you first to see if there was some sort of protocol in place when it's a child in the care system.'

She explained that some support staff and the school caretaker were currently walking round the outside perimeter of the school grounds to see if they could see Nancy in the nearby streets.

'I need to call her social worker immediately and tell her what's happened and she'll take a view from there,' I told her, feeling sick. 'Do you know what made her run away like that?'

'I asked her friends and her teacher but they couldn't think of anything in particular,' she said. 'I'm really sorry, Maggie. I hoped that I had made it clear to Nancy that if she was upset or worried about something that she could come and see me.'

'It's nobody's fault,' I told her. 'She's eleven. If she really wanted to leave school, she would have found a way.'

I could hear that she was genuinely concerned.

'I'm going to hang up now,' I told her. 'But please give me a call if she turns up.'

'I will do,' she said. 'And again I'm sorry about all of this.'

As I called Juliet and explained what had happened, my chest tightened with worry.

'Considering how vulnerable she is at the moment, I'm really concerned that she managed to get out like that,' sighed Juliet.

But I knew that was a conversation we needed to have later with the school. Our priority now was to find Nancy and make sure that she was OK.

Juliet was a very level-headed person and calm in a crisis.

'I'm going to ring the police,' she told me. 'And then I'll head to the school.'

'Do you want me to meet you there?' I asked her.

'No, you stay at home just in case Nancy turns up.'

Worryingly, I knew Nancy wouldn't have a clue how to get from school to my house as I'd always driven her and it was such a long way.

'I hope she's all right,' I sighed.

'Maggie, we will find her,' she reassured me. 'She's not the first child to have gone missing from school and she won't be the last.'

That was true but after everything that had happened in her life recently, the idea of a vulnerable eleven-year-old wandering the streets terrified me.

'OK, let's keep in touch,' I told her.

I spent the next hour pacing the house and worrying. At times like these I felt really helpless because there was nothing I could do. I wracked my brains trying to think of where Nancy might have gone. Had she tried to get to the prison to see her mum? But she'd been so adamant that she didn't want to see her. Plus it was an incredibly long way away and she wouldn't know how to get there on public transport. Maybe she'd just gone to the local park to clear her head and would turn up at school later?

So many scenarios were running through my head and the thought of something happening to her on my watch was unbearable.

After an hour, I hadn't heard anything more from Juliet so I texted her to see if there was any news.

Nothing. The police are aware and I'm about to head to the school and meet them there.

A few seconds later, my mobile rang and I leapt on it.

'Maggie, it's DC Hayley Hirst,' said a voice.

'Oh hi Hayley,' I said, assuming she was ringing to update me about the court case.

'I've just had a phone call from one of Nancy and Helen's neighbours. Apparently, she's just found Nancy sitting outside her old house crying.'

My heart sank with relief. I knew her old house was only a fifteen-minute walk from school, so she hadn't gone far.

'Thank goodness,' I sighed. 'She walked out of school over an hour ago. We've called the police and everyone is out looking for her.'

She explained that the neighbour, Eleanor, had DC Hirst's number from when they were doing door-to-door inquiries after Martin was stabbed.

'Is Nancy OK?' I asked.

'She's apparently very upset but the neighbour has taken her into her house so she's safe but she's been asking for you.'

'Thank you so much,' I told her. 'I'll call Juliet now.'

Juliet was just getting into her car when I rang.

'Gosh, what a relief,' she sighed. 'If I let the school know she's been found then are you OK to go and pick her up?'

'Yes of course,' I said. 'I'll set off now.'

'Keep me posted,' she replied. 'And I'll pop round later to see how she is.'

As I drove to Nancy's old house, I felt an overwhelming sense of relief. Whatever had happened or however Nancy was feeling, we could sort it and talk it through. She was safe now and that was all that mattered.

CHAPTER TEN

Forward Planning

I knocked on the door and waited. The house was another huge detached property, similar to Nancy's family home. A few seconds later it was opened by a blonde woman who looked to be in her fifties. She was casually but expensively dressed, with immaculately styled hair.

'I'm Nancy's foster carer, Maggie Hartley,' I told her, flashing her my ID. 'Hopefully you're expecting me?'

'Yes of course,' she smiled. 'The policewoman called me back and said you were coming. I'm Eleanor. Come on in.'

I stepped into a large hallway that had a huge sweeping staircase and a large chandelier suspended from the vaulted ceiling. A little white poodle was running around her feet.

'This is Teddy,' she told me. 'I was out walking him when I passed the house and saw Nancy. Poor little mite was sat on the ground by the front door, absolutely sobbing her heart out. I brought her in here and got her a juice but she's still very upset. I'm not surprised after everything that's happened,' she whispered. 'Such a terrible business.'

'Thank you so much,' I told her. 'I'm so relieved that you found her. We were all terribly worried.'

Eleanor walked me through to a large kitchen at the back of the house overlooking the garden. Nancy was sat at the breakfast bar, her eyes red and puffy. When she saw me, tears started streaming down her face.

'I'll leave you two to have a chat,' said Eleanor kindly.

'Thank you,' I said.

I went over to Nancy and wrapped my arms around her and she cuddled into my chest.

'It's OK,' I soothed. 'You let it all out.'

She stayed like that for a good ten minutes, crying until she had no more tears left.

'I'm sorry,' she sighed.

'What happened?' I asked her gently. 'We were all so worried about you. Why did you leave school?'

'Everyone was talking and whispering about me,' she gulped. 'They were saying my mum had killed my dad. And I tried not to get upset and ignore them but I'd had enough.'

She started to cry again.

'But do you know what the saddest thing is? They're right. What they're saying is all true. Why did she do it, Maggie? Why did she hurt him?'

She buried her face into my shoulder and sobbed. In all honesty I couldn't answer her question so I didn't try to. All I could do was hold her and let her cry it out in the hope that she'd get some release and feel better afterwards.

Eventually Nancy started to calm down and Eleanor came back into the kitchen to make us all a cup of tea.

'There's no rush,' she smiled. 'You can stay here as long as you want.'

'Thank you, Mrs Fuller,' Nancy said.

'Just call me Eleanor, darling,' she replied.

While Nancy stayed in the kitchen with Eleanor, I went out into the hallway to call Juliet and update her.

'I think the whispering and pointing at school all got a bit too much for her,' I told her. 'She's OK but she's very upset.'

We agreed that I would take her straight home.

'I've spoken to the school and filled them in,' Juliet told me.

When I went back into the kitchen, Nancy was sat on the floor playing with Teddy.

'You can take him out into the garden and throw his ball to him if you'd like?' suggested Eleanor. 'He loves that.'

'Yes please,' replied Nancy, smiling for the first time in what felt like days.

As she ran out into the garden after an excited Teddy, Eleanor and I sipped our tea.

'My heart breaks for her,' she sighed. 'It's been such a shock.'

'Did you know the family well?' I asked.

'I've lived next door to them for ten years but I can't say I do,' she told me. 'Helen was always very polite but they generally kept themselves to themselves. Nancy loves the dog so I often invited her round to come and play with him but she never did.'

'What was Mr Miller like?' I asked her.

'Quite serious and not particularly friendly but, to be honest, I hardly saw him. They seemed like a very close-knit kind of family. They never had visitors over and I never saw any cars in the driveway.'

She described how the whole street had been in shock about what had happened.

'There were a couple of odd things over the years but nothing that suggested anything was seriously wrong. I didn't hear any shouting or arguments or see the police there.'

'What sort of odd things?' I asked, interested.

'Oh it was a few years ago now,' sighed Eleanor. 'I remember it was a cold winter's night. It was pouring with rain and blowing a hooley out there. The Millers have a security light in the corner of their garden and when it lights up, I can see it in my bedroom at the back of the house.'

She explained that she had gone to bed one night and she'd noticed the light was on for a while.

'I thought it was probably a fox or a cat but I thought I'd have a look outside just in case,' she told me. 'But when I looked, Helen was standing in the garden; she had no shoes on and just a little flimsy nightdress. It was a freezing cold night and it was pouring down but she was just stood there, as still as a statue, on the patio.'

Eleanor said she had knocked on the window to get Helen's attention.

'I wanted to make sure she was OK,' she told me. 'I was worried that she'd get hypothermia being out like that.'

She described how Helen had looked up but she didn't say anything.

'I'm sure she'd seen me but she didn't say a word. She just carried on standing there. It was all very strange but when I checked half an hour later, she'd gone.'

She described another time when she'd bumped into Helen in the queue for the till at the local shop and Helen was in tears.

'She'd looked into her purse and realised she didn't have enough money to pay for her shopping,' Eleanor told me.

The cashier had suggested that she paid with a card.

'Nancy was with her,' she explained. 'She must have been around seven or eight and I remember her saying, "Daddy doesn't let Mummy have cards." I thought that was really strange given all the money they seemed to have.'

'I remember when I offered to pay for her shopping, she seemed so relieved and grateful,' Eleanor added. 'She thanked me and said she would be in trouble because she'd spent all her allowance. I mean, with a lovely big house and cars like that, I can't imagine for one second they were struggling for money,' she told me. 'But having an allowance seemed like something my mother would have had in the fifties. Surely if she needed more money for shopping then Martin would have just given it to her? It was a few years ago now but I remember thinking at the time it was all a bit odd.'

'Did you tell the police any of this?' I asked.

'No,' she shrugged. 'I've only just remembered and it didn't seem relevant. They were asking what I'd seen and heard on the night Martin got killed. This was years ago now. I think they were just one of those couples who've been together for years and were very dependent on each other,' Eleanor told me. 'Mind you, I'm divorced so I'm not the best person to comment on other people's relationships.'

It niggled at me, but I thought she was probably right about the couple being co-dependent. The incidents she'd mentioned were only small things that had happened years ago and probably weren't relevant to the current police investigation.

Nancy eventually came in from the garden and after finishing our tea, we said goodbye and thanked Eleanor.

'You take care, darling,' she told Nancy. 'And if you ever need anything, you know where I am.'

'Thank you,' she replied. 'And I'm sorry for worrying everybody.'

In the car on the way home, Nancy and I chatted.

'I'm going to take you home now but Juliet and I would both like you to go back to school tomorrow,' I told her.

Her face crumpled.

'But what if people are saying things again and talking about me?'

'Miss Judd is going to have another word with the girls today and explain how upset you are,' I told her. 'And all of the teachers are going to be looking out for you to try to make sure that the other girls don't worry you. But the fact is, Nancy, people might say things. I know it's hard and it's upsetting, but you can't let other people stop you from going to school. I promise you that soon they'll have other things to talk about.'

It felt like I was being harsh but I couldn't pretend that it wasn't going to happen. Children were going to talk because they'd hear their parents talking about it or they'd hear about the case on the news.

It was also approaching the end of June and Nancy only had a few weeks left of school before they broke up for the summer holidays. I felt it was important for her to go back in otherwise it would be an even bigger wrench come September.

The following day she was still reluctant but she went in as we'd asked.

'I'm so proud of you,' I told her as I dropped her off. 'You're being really brave.'

I was also keen for her to go back to school because a couple of days later, we had her Looked After Child (LAC) review. This was something that was held within two to three weeks of any child coming into the care system. It was a chance for everyone involved in a child's care to get together and share information and work out where we were and what the long- or short-term plan might be.

Sometimes LAC reviews would be held at my house but because there would be quite a few people attending this one, I was relieved when Juliet suggested that we all meet at the Social Services building in town. Miss Judd had been invited along as well as DC Hirst; there would also be Juliet and Becky, and it felt like there would be too many people to try to squeeze into my living room.

It was also a chance for me to meet Nancy's Independent Reviewing Officer, or IRO as they are known. This was someone who worked for Social Services but who wasn't directly involved in the case who could represent Nancy and make sure that all her needs were being met. Nancy's IRO was a man called Colin Brown.

It was unusual to have a male IRO as generally speaking, most of the social workers I tended to come across were women. Colin was the first person I met as I walked into the meeting room at Social Services. I was surprised to find a man in his thirties as his name had suggested someone older.

'Nice to meet you, Maggie,' he said, giving my hand a very firm and enthusiastic handshake.

He was very cheerful and friendly and I instantly liked him.

One by one, everyone else arrived and he introduced himself before he started to chair the meeting.

'Firstly, massive apologies are due as I haven't actually had the chance to meet Nancy yet,' he told us. 'But that's something I will be doing this week and I'll liaise with Maggie about that after this meeting.'

Then Colin invited DC Hirst to update everyone on where the criminal proceedings were at. She explained that Helen had been charged with murder and in another few weeks would appear at court to enter a plea. If she pleaded not guilty then there would be a trial, which could take up to a year to go to court, or if she pleaded guilty then sentencing would be a lot quicker and she could be back in court in a matter of weeks or a few months. Either way, it was all very unknown at the present time.

They had also contacted Helen's parents in France.

'We informed them about what had happened, which has understandably been a huge shock to them,' she told us. 'They haven't seen Helen or been in touch with her for well over twelve years and they didn't know they had a granddaughter.

'They've given me permission to pass on their details to Social Services so they can carry on that conversation.'

Juliet nodded.

'Unfortunately, myself and Helen's parents are playing phone tag at the minute,' Juliet explained 'I've tried to call them and they've left a couple of messages for me so I'm hoping to catch up with them this week.'

DC Hirst explained that when Nancy, Juliet and I had visited the prison there hadn't been a huge amount of time to talk to Helen but that she had been liaising with the prison social worker who'd had regular conversations with Helen.

'We wanted to find out if there were any family members or friends who could look after Nancy under the kinship care scheme,' she told us. 'Helen didn't believe that there was.'

She'd told the prison social worker that she was estranged from her parents and hadn't seen them since she had come to England as a teenager and met Mr Miller.

'As Hayley has already said, they've never met Nancy. But when I get hold of them, I will obviously talk everything through with them.' Juliet continued

Colin was busy taking notes.

'What about Mr Miller's parents?' he asked. 'Could they be possible candidates for kinship care?'

DC Hirst shook her head.

'Mr Miller was estranged from his parents and unfortunately they're both now dead. We have been in touch with his brother who has hasn't seen him since he was a teenager.'

She described how he hadn't wanted to come and identify his brother's body and didn't want his details passed on to Social Services.

'Gosh, there is obviously a lot of animosity there for some reason,' Colin remarked.

No one knew what went on with families but it was both odd and heartbreaking that Martin's own brother wanted nothing to do with him even after his death.

The situation as it stood was that Helen had agreed to a Section 20, which meant that she had given her permission for Nancy to stay in the care system so Social Services didn't have to apply for a court order.

'We obviously need to wait and see what happens with regards to any court case to know what the long-term situation is going to be,' said Juliet. 'I know Maggie is happy to continue with the placement until we have an outcome.'

I nodded in agreement.

DC Hirst also had another update.

'I heard from the coroner this morning that Mr Miller's body is being released for burial early next week,' she told us.

'In the absence of any family, Mr Miller's business partner and friend, Dominic Moss, has agreed to take on the arrangements for the funeral so he will be handling that.'

My heart sank at the thought of a funeral because it was another thing for Nancy to cope with. Funerals were never easy for anyone, especially a child, but it was important that she was given the opportunity to say goodbye.

Then it was Miss Judd's turn to update us about school.

'We had a blip the other day when she ran away from school which I'm sure you're all aware of,' she said. 'But since then things have settled down and Nancy seems to be a lot happier.'

She was going to be starting sessions with the school counsellor and they'd also nominated two members of staff who Nancy could go to during the school day if she was feeling overwhelmed.

'I think break times have been particularly hard for her, so she knows she can go to their classrooms for some time out if she needs it,' she added.

'What about the next academic year?' asked Colin. 'Is she going to be going back to the same school in September?'

'Yes,' nodded Miss Judd. 'Our school caters for girls up to the age of thirteen and Mr Miller was always very prompt at paying the fees.

'In fact, talking to our bursar, the entire academic year for next year has already been paid for in full.'

There was no way Social Services would be able to cover private school fees so it was a relief to know Nancy wouldn't have to change schools and face more upheaval.

Finally it was my turn to address the meeting.

'There's not a huge amount to say,' I shrugged. 'Over the three weeks she's been with me, Nancy has settled in well. She's a lovely girl – very polite and tidy.'

I described the prison visit and the upset that it had caused her.

'It's not surprising really,' added Juliet. 'I think we're all struggling to understand what led Helen to do what she did.'

I also talked about how school had been a bit up and down but that Miss Judd had been very supportive and that it was getting easier for Nancy.

'Understandably she just feels very lost – her whole world has been turned upside down and the people she loved have been taken away from her.'

As I spoke, Colin was writing all this down.

'I think all we can do is reconvene in three months when we'll hopefully know more about what's happening with regards to any criminal proceedings,' he said.

If Helen either pleaded guilty or was found guilty of murder, she was facing a very long prison sentence and Nancy was facing the rest of her childhood in the care system. It was a sobering thought and I left the meeting not feeling any clearer about the long-term plan for Nancy. No one had any answers and the next few weeks were going to be challenging for her with her dad's funeral and potentially finding out if her mum was going to plead guilty or not. All we could do was take it one step at a time.

CHAPTER ELEVEN

Decisions

A few days later, I had a phone call.

'Hello, it's Dominic here,' said a hesitant voice. 'Dominic Moss. I'm Martin Miller's business partner and friend.'

'Oh hello,' I said. 'Juliet said she'd given you my number and that you'd be calling.'

He explained that he was organising Martin's funeral and wanted to talk to Nancy about what she thought her dad would have liked.

'I thought she might want to get involved in helping me plan the service,' he said.

'We haven't actually talked to her about the funeral yet,' I replied. 'I was waiting until I'd spoken to you.'

It was being held in a couple of weeks at a local church.

'Martin wasn't really a churchgoer but I know he wanted to be buried and there's room in the cemetery there for him.'

'It's really good of you to take all of this on,' I told him. 'It can't be easy.'

'It's not something I ever thought I'd be doing but in the

absence of anyone else, I agreed to help out,' he sighed. 'I couldn't bear for him to have to be buried by the council. I still can't believe what's happened, to be honest.'

He sounded really shaken.

I explained that although Juliet and I were of the belief that it was good for older children to attend funerals to try to give them some sense of closure, we wanted to give Nancy the choice.

'We don't want her to feel like she's being forced to go,' I told him. 'It might simply be too much for her at this point.'

I also agreed that I thought it would be nice for her to feel involved in the planning.

'She is only eleven though so I don't think she should be choosing things like coffins,' I told him. 'But she might like to pick some flowers or decide on a poem or a reading for the service.'

'Of course,' he replied. 'I don't have kids myself but I completely understand. I don't want to upset her after everything she's been through.'

Dominic suggested that he call back one afternoon when Nancy was home from school so he could have a chat with her.

'My feeling is that Nancy would be able to cope with it better if you were able to come round and talk to her in person rather than on the phone,' I told him.

'OK,' he said.

We decided that Juliet and I would talk to Nancy over the next few days then let him know how she reacted.

I was apprehensive about talking to her about the funeral. She'd had so much to cope with recently and school had all felt like too much, so I wasn't sure how she was going to react.

117

Juliet wasn't able to make it round that afternoon but she came the following day after school.

'Nancy, I wanted to chat to you about something,' she told her. 'When someone dies, people tend to have a funeral for them so that they can pay their respects and there's going to be one for your dad soon.'

'A funeral?' she asked, looking surprised.

I don't think the thought of a funeral had even crossed her mind.

'Have you been to a funeral before?' I asked her and she shook her head.

'It's an opportunity for friends and family to come together and say goodbye,' I added. 'It's very sad but at the same time, it's nice for people to talk and remember that person and the happy times that you shared with them.'

'I haven't been to one but I know what one is,' she replied.

I explained that it was being arranged by her dad's business partner Dominic.

'Because your mummy is in prison, she's not able to make any of the arrangements, so Dominic, who used to work with your daddy, is going to sort it all out.'

'Do you remember him?' Juliet asked her and she nodded. Do you know him well?'

'Not really,' she shrugged. 'I know he's Daddy's friend at work but Mummy and I didn't really see him a lot.'

'What do you think?' I asked her. 'Do you think you'd like to go?'

I could see her mulling things over in her mind.

'Will Daddy have a grave?' she asked me.

'Yes, I think he is going to be buried,' I told her. 'But that's something you can talk to Dominic about.'

'Dominic thought you might like to help him choose some flowers and some music for the service,' Juliet told her. 'If you wanted, you could help him pick things your daddy liked.'

'You don't have to go to the funeral if you don't want to,' I reassured her. 'We're not going to make you but we wanted to tell you about it and give you the choice. But whatever you decide, Juliet and I will be here to support you.'

Nancy looked deep in thought.

'Is Mummy going to be there?' she asked.

I looked at Juliet as that was something I didn't know the answer to.

'At this stage, I honestly don't know, Nancy,' replied Juliet. 'I need to talk to Mummy's social worker at the prison to see what she thinks.'

'I don't want her to go,' she frowned. 'It's not fair. She was the one who hurt Daddy – she shouldn't be allowed to say goodbye.'

'I can understand why you feel that way but unfortunately it's not our decision,' Juliet told her. 'It's up to the prison to decide.'

We agreed that Nancy could think about it over the next few days and she would let us know what she wanted to do when she was ready. Once I knew her decision then I could get back to Dominic.

I didn't want Nancy to feel under any pressure so I didn't talk about the funeral or mention it for the rest of the evening. Although I believed that it was helpful for children to go to the funeral when a loved one died, it was going to be hard and upsetting for her and it might not be what she needed after everything else that she'd been through.

That night I was tucking her into bed after she'd had a bath.

'Night night, flower,' I told her, giving her a hug. 'See you in the morning.'

'Will Daddy be in a coffin?' she asked me suddenly.

She'd obviously been going over things in her mind.

'Yes,' I nodded. 'Your dad's body will be in a coffin at the front of the church.'

'Will I have to see him?' she asked.

'No, sweetie, not if you don't want to,' I reassured her. 'The coffin is closed so you can't see what's inside.'

'Will they dig a big hole in the ground and put him in it?' she asked.

I was a big believer in being honest and telling children the truth and Nancy seemed genuinely inquisitive rather than upset.

'Yes, if he's being buried then that's what they'll do,' I told her. 'First there will be a service in the church and then afterwards Daddy will be buried in the cemetery outside.'

I explained how there wouldn't be a gravestone at first but after several months, when the ground had settled, we could get a stone slab and Nancy could help choose what was written on it.

'I don't want the funeral to cause you any worry,' I told her. 'You don't have to go if you don't want to and you don't have to make a decision right now.'

She shook her head and suddenly sat up in bed.

'No,' she said firmly. 'I've already decided. I want to go. I want to say bye to Daddy.'

'OK,' I smiled. 'I'll let Juliet know and then Dominic can come round and have a chat with you.'

I knew it couldn't have been an easy decision for her to make and I was really proud of her.

She hadn't asked about her mum again but we still didn't know whether Helen wanted to come or even if she was allowed to.

A couple of days later, Dominic came round. He was a portly man in his forties but very well dressed in a designer suit and he smelled of expensive aftershave. I could tell he was nervous as I invited him into the living room where Nancy was sitting.

'Gosh, you've grown since I last saw you,' he told her.

Nancy was very quiet and shy around him and I could tell that she didn't know him well.

I'd asked Dominic to bring all the information from the funeral directors so he could show Nancy a picture of the coffin. I wanted her to be prepared for what would happen on the day.

I left them to talk while I went into the kitchen to make us all a cup of tea. When I came back, they were chatting away and Nancy seemed more interested than upset.

'I've seen the coffin, Maggie,' she told me matter-of-factly. 'It's a wooden one with shiny gold handles. Dominic says it's going to be very heavy for the funeral men to carry.'

'Yes, it probably will be,' I said.

'We haven't got very far with the music,' he added.

'Daddy didn't like music or singing,' nodded Nancy. 'He liked things nice and quiet.'

But she had chosen some flowers to go on top of the coffin.

'I picked red and yellow roses and I want it to spell out DADDY so everyone knows that it's from me,' she said proudly.

'That's lovely,' I smiled.

She seemed remarkably upbeat about it all and the serious-ness of the day didn't seem to have really hit her yet.

'Maggie, please can I go to the toilet?' she asked me.

'Of course you can, lovey,' I told her. 'You know by now that you don't need to ask permission. You just go.'

I was quite pleased to have a few minutes to talk to Dominic on my own.

'She's as polite as ever,' he smiled. 'I know Martin was very keen on manners.'

'You were obviously very close to him,' I replied. 'It must be hard.'

'Martin and I worked together for many years but I can't say we spent a lot of time together outside of work,' he sighed. 'He was a very private person. I know his family meant the world to him though and he was devoted to Helen and Nancy. He couldn't wait to get home to them at the end of the day.'

He shook his head.

'I still can't get my head around what happened,' he sighed. 'I just don't understand it. I don't know Helen well but she seemed like a nice, quiet woman.'

He seemed as confused as everyone else about what had happened.

'Have you been in contact with her?' I asked him.

'I called the prison and arranged to speak to her,' he told me. 'I felt she should be involved in making some of the decisions about the funeral.' Even though she was accused of murdering Martin, Helen was still his next of kin.

'And what did she say?' I asked, curious.

'She just cried down the phone,' he said. 'She was obviously upset and I couldn't get anything out of her.'

Dominic was also trying to help sort out their financial affairs.

'They don't have a mortgage on the house and Nancy's school fees have been paid for the foreseeable,' he explained. 'But if she ever needs anything then please let me know.'

'Thank you,' I said as he handed me his business card.

'What will happen to her if Helen goes to prison?' he asked.

'At this stage, we don't know,' I sighed. 'We need to see what happens with the court case really before any decisions are made.'

A few seconds later, Nancy walked back into the room.

'I was just saying to Maggie if you need anything then please let me know,' he told her. 'And thank you for all your help,' he added. 'I bet your dad would be very proud of you.'

'That's OK,' she said, her eyes filling with tears.

It was the first time that I'd seen her upset all day.

The following morning I called Juliet to update her about Dominic's visit.

'I've just heard from the prison social worker,' she told me. 'Helen does want to go to the funeral.'

'Really?' I gasped. 'Are you allowed to go to the funeral of someone that you're accused of killing?'

'It's at the prison's discretion whether they give permission or not,' she replied. 'And if she goes, it would be with an escort.'

I had conflicting opinions. On the one hand, Martin had been her husband so she perhaps had the right to say goodbye. On the other, it looked like she was the one responsible for taking his life and I didn't want to put Nancy through the ordeal of seeing her mum standing by her dad's grave in handcuffs.

'It's already going to be an emotional day for Nancy and I think if Helen was there, it would just make her even more upset and angry ,' I told her.

She was still adamant that she never wanted to see her mother again and she refused to talk about it.

Juliet could pass on how Nancy felt to the prison social worker but we couldn't influence that decision.

Over the next week, Nancy and I chatted about the funeral. I wanted to prepare her as best I could, talk her through what would happen and let her know that it was OK to ask any questions. As there wasn't any other family besides Nancy attending, there were no funeral cars and I'd arranged to drive Nancy to the church. I explained what would happen at the service.

'You'll sit right at the front because you're family,' I told her. 'And Daddy's coffin will be there, which Dominic showed you a picture of.'

She nodded, taking it all in.

'Will you sit with me?' she asked.

'Of course,' I nodded. 'And Juliet will be there too.'

I prepared her for the fact that some people would get upset.

'Some people will be very sad and they might cry and you might feel very upset too,' I told her. 'But that's OK. And if it all gets too much for you then squeeze my hand three times and I'll know that's our signal that you want to leave.'

She nodded and seemed relieved to have a back-up plan.

I was serving up dinner later when she wandered downstairs and put something on the kitchen table.

'What's that, lovey?' I asked as I dished out some carrots.

'It's a card for Daddy,' she told me. 'Dominic said I could give him something to put in his coffin that Daddy could take to heaven with him.'

I was surprised as I hadn't heard that conversation.

'That's a lovely idea,' I smiled. 'Would you mind if we had a look at it?'

She shook her head.

I'm sorry Mummy did this to you. I love you Daddy. We are nothing without you. Have a nice time in heaven.

'It's really beautiful,' I told her. 'I'll give Dominic a ring and make sure that he passes it on to the undertakers.'

As the day of the funeral drew closer, we also had to pick out something for Nancy to wear.

She'd already decided with Dominic that she wanted people to wear bright colours and she had plenty of lovely clothes so I didn't feel it was necessary to buy anything new.

'Have you decided what you want to wear to the funeral?' I asked her one afternoon after school.

She opened up her wardrobe and started to flick through the rails.

'It's so hard to choose,' she sighed. 'Daddy would always pick our clothes.'

'Your clothes?' I asked her.

'And Mummy's too,' she nodded. 'He liked us to look smart. Mummy didn't know what to wear so Daddy always decided.'

'Wow, that's unusual,' I sighed. 'Most men I know aren't very good at picking clothes.'

'He bought all of Mummy's clothes too,' Nancy told me. 'Otherwise she would pick the wrong things and she would look like a tart.'

At first I thought I must have misheard her.

'Sorry Nancy, say that again,' I asked her.

'Daddy chose Mummy's clothes so she didn't look like a tart,' she repeated.

'Tart' was such a strange word to hear coming out of this well-spoken child's mouth, I was completely taken aback.

'What does "tart" mean?' I asked her.

'Oh that's when your clothes don't look nice,' she told me. 'Mummy needed Daddy to show her the ones she was allowed to wear.'

'Well I don't like that word so let's not use it here,' I said calmly.

It was a really odd thing for her to say and I recorded it in the notes that I sent to Becky at the end of every day. Part of working for an agency was that I did daily recordings to try to build up a picture of a child; Becky would then send a monthly summary to Juliet, who would pick up on anything that concerned her.

As the funeral edged closer, the one thing preying on my mind was whether Helen was going to attend. Nancy hadn't asked about her mum since we first spoke at the funeral. but I was dreading the question. If her mum was coming then I wanted her to have prior warning and it also might mean that she didn't want to go any more.

I knew that Juliet was trying to get hold of the prison social worker to get a definitive answer. The afternoon before the service, she rang me.

'I've finally got through to them and Helen's not coming,' she told me.

'Thank goodness the prison saw sense,' I sighed.

'I don't think it was the prison. It was Helen who decided to withdraw her request to come.'

Even though she'd been accused of murder, I felt so sad for Helen. She'd lost her husband and her daughter and no matter what she'd done or why, that can't have been easy for her.

As soon as Nancy had finished school (because Maggie usually picked her up), I told her the news.

'Juliet rang me and let me know that the prison has been in touch to say Mummy isn't coming to the funeral tomorrow.'

'I'm glad they won't let her come,' she said.

'Actually, it was your mum who decided that she wasn't going to come,' I told her.

'Good,' she sighed.

We didn't talk any more about the funeral until bedtime.

'Tomorrow's going to be a long day so try to get some sleep,' I told her gently. 'And remember what we said – if you change your mind at any point then you don't have to go. Even when we're there, if it all gets a bit much for you, you can squeeze my hand and we'll leave.'

'I want to go,' she told me. 'I want to say goodbye to Daddy.'

I just hoped that the day was going to go smoothly and that Nancy was going to be able to cope.

CHAPTER TWELVE

The Hardest Goodbye

As we walked into the church, I reached for Nancy's hand and gave it a squeeze.

'Are you OK?' I asked her.

She nodded but I could see a nervous look in her eyes. Juliet and Dominic were waiting for us at the back of the church.

'Hi Nancy,' smiled Dominic, who was dressed in a smart suit. 'You look lovely.'

'Thank you,' she said shyly, looking down at the pink and white dress that she'd eventually chosen the night before.

We must have been earlier than I thought because there were only five or six people in the church. I could see that Martin's coffin was already in place at the front.

'Can we go and sit down, Maggie?' whispered Nancy, tugging on my sleeve.

'I'll wait here to greet people as they come in,' Dominic told us.

Juliet and I walked to the front with Nancy. Juliet went into the pew first, followed by Nancy then I sat in the seat nearest to the aisle right next to the coffin. I could see Nancy staring at it.

'Is that really Daddy?' she whispered.

'Yes, flower,' I told her. 'Remember we talked about how Daddy's body would be in there.'

But rather than being upset, she seemed more curious than anything.

'Your flowers look really beautiful,' I told her.

On the top of Martin's coffin were two arrangements. One was Nancy's – DADDY spelt out in roses. The other was a little wreath of pink roses. I was close enough that I could read the card on them.

I'm so sorry Martin. Love you forever, Helen xx

It was such a loving message and it was hard to believe that it had come from the woman accused of his murder. None of us knew what to think and it was all still so mystifying.

Nancy turned and looked around the church.

'I don't know any of these people,' she muttered.

I glanced at my watch. There were only a few minutes to go until the service started but the church wasn't even a quarter full. When someone had died young and so tragically like Martin, I'd expected the place to be packed but there was only about twenty people there. The only people I recognised were DC Hirst and Eleanor, Nancy's next-door neighbour.

The service was short and it was obvious that the vicar hadn't known Martin. Dominic stood up and said a few words, mainly about his work achievements.

'He was also a devoted father to Nancy,' he said, looking up and smiling across at her. 'There's nothing he loved more than spending time at home with his family.'

I put my arm around her and she gave me a weak smile. No one mentioned Helen at all.

It was a relief when the organ started playing and the service was over. Thankfully Nancy seemed to be holding up OK.

We wandered out of the church and into the graveyard.

'Is this the bit where he gets buried in the ground?' she asked and I nodded.

While we waited for Martin's coffin to be carried out of the church, people came over to Nancy to say how sorry they were. Most of them seemed to be from Martin's work or were neighbours from their street who had come to pay their respects. There were no friends or relatives.

Once the coffin was in place, we all gathered around the grave. I put my arm around Nancy and as the vicar began to talk, I could feel her body shaking.

'It's OK,' I soothed. 'I'm right here.'

That's when the tears started to fall. I couldn't hear what the vicar was saying as I was completely focused on Nancy. As Martin's coffin was lowered into the ground and the final prayers were said, her tears turned into loud, gulping, hysterical sobs.

'I m-miss you, Daddy,' she gasped. 'It's n-not f-fair.'

She was getting more and more distressed and I was worried her legs were going to collapse beneath her. I glanced at Juliet and we both seemed to be thinking now was the right time to lead her away.

'Come on sweetie,' I soothed. 'Let's go for a walk.'

We managed to usher her over to the other side of the churchyard where we found a bench. I sat down next to her and she curled up in my arms.

'It's n-not fair,' she sobbed, her lips quivering. 'I can't believe I'll n-never see h-him again.'

I think the harsh reality of seeing her dad's coffin being lowered into the earth had brought home what had happened and it had suddenly hit her that he really was gone.

I felt utterly powerless to help her. It was hard seeing a child so distressed but this was one of those times when I couldn't say anything to make it better. She was grieving and all I could do was let her cry it out and be there to hold her and make her feel as safe and reassured as I could.

A few minutes later, Dominic came over to us.

'How's she doing?' he asked.

'I think it all got a bit too much for her,' Juliet told him.

We'd already agreed we didn't think it was a good idea for her to go to the wake, which was just a few sandwiches in the church hall.

'She's very upset and I think it's best if I take her straight home,' I told him.

'I understand,' he nodded.

Juliet helped me lead Nancy to the car. She'd stopped crying and looked drained.

'That must have been so hard for you, Nancy, but you were really brave,' Juliet told her. 'It was a lovely goodbye for your dad.'

She nodded.

'I hope she's OK,' Juliet told me as I got into the car. 'Keep in touch.'

On the way back, I chit-chatted to Nancy in the car. I talked about silly, mundane things but I thought it might be comforting for her to know what was going to happen when we got home.

'Let's go back and get some lunch,' I told her. 'I'll make you a sandwich so have a think about what you fancy. I've got some chicken or some ham and I've got some of those prawn cocktail crisps that you like.

'I think we could both do with a peaceful afternoon. So you could watch a film or read your book.'

When we got home, I made her try to eat something even though she wasn't keen. Afterwards, I put a film on for her but she kept appearing in the kitchen where I was tidying up and I could tell that she wanted to be near me.

'Do you want me to come and watch it with you?' I suggested and she nodded.

Even though it was a warm summer's day outside, we curled up on the sofa together and I could tell Nancy was craving that closeness and reassurance.

Afterwards I suggested that we did some baking. I thought it was a nice calming activity to do together and it would help to take Nancy's mind off things. She seemed to be really enjoying it as she helped me measure out the ingredients and mix it all together.

'Give it forty-five minutes and we should be able to tuck in,' I smiled as I put the sponge in the oven.

'Oh no, you can't eat cake, Maggie,' she told me. 'It makes you fat and if you're fat no one will ever want you.'

It was such a strange thing to say and I was astonished.

'Who told you that, sweetie?' I asked her casually.

'That's what I heard Daddy say to Mummy,' she told me. 'He didn't want Mummy to get fat so she wasn't allowed cake or biscuits or sweets. It's not nice to be fat is it, Maggie? No one will want you then.'

I wasn't quite sure what to say in response to that.

'Well I like to eat cake,' I told her. 'It doesn't matter if you're fat or thin. If somebody loves you, then they love you for you.'

'Well Daddy loved Mummy so much and that's why he didn't want her to be fat.'

One or two of the things Nancy had said recently were starting to bother me. Again, I wrote it in my daily notes and reminded myself to have a chat with Becky about it and get her thoughts.

But now my main focus was getting Nancy through today.

At bedtime she was really quiet.

'I'm so proud of you,' I told her. 'I know today must have been so hard for you.'

'I wanted to do it for Daddy,' she replied. 'To say goodbye.'

'Well, you helped to give him a lovely goodbye,' I smiled.

I explained that we could go up to the grave whenever she wanted.

'You can take him flowers and still talk to him,' I told her.

'But he can't hear me,' she replied, looking puzzled.

'It's nice to have a place where you can go to feel close to your dad,' I said. 'Or you can remember him in your head. It's up to you and what you feel like doing. Everyone is different and different things bring them comfort.'

She nodded, taking it all in.

'Do I have to go to school tomorrow?' she asked as she snuggled down under the duvet.

'Juliet and I talked about it and we think it's a good idea,' I told her.

I thought it would be good for her to return to her normal routine as soon as possible. The main thing that keeps children stable is familiarity and having a routine. If she woke up in the morning very distraught and in floods of tears, then of course I wouldn't send her, but I believed that having a structure of lessons and seeing her friends would do her good.

In the morning, she seemed a little tired but she wasn't tearful and she headed off to school without any objections. I'd just got home when Becky rang to say she was popping by for a cup of tea.

'I'm sorry I haven't met Nancy yet,' she told me. 'Things have been manic but I wanted to see how you were doing.'

I told her about the funeral and everything that had happened over the past few weeks since the LAC review.

'Have you been reading my notes?' I asked her.

I told her about the conversation that we'd had about her dad choosing her mum's clothes, the way she'd used the word 'tart' and the comment last night about the cakes.

'There are just a few odd things that she's been saying,' I told her.

'She might just have overheard things wrongly or got the wrong end of the stick about things,' Becky told me. 'You know how kids are.'

'Maybe,' I sighed, but I couldn't help but wonder if I was slowly building up a true picture of how things had been at home.

'There was actually something else I wanted to talk to you about,' said Becky. 'How would you feel about taking on another placement?'

I wasn't expecting this and it took me completely by surprise, although as a foster carer, it was rare to just have one placement like I did at present.

'How many children is it?' I asked.

'Just the one,' she replied.

She explained that it was a three-year-old boy called Sid.

'Unfortunately, his eight-year-old brother, Fred, has severe epilepsy and can have up to a hundred seizures a day,' she told me.

Doctors wanted to do an operation on his brain to see if it would help reduce the number and the severity of them.

'Jo – the boys' mum – is a single parent,' she explained. 'All her family are in Poland and she has no other support network that can help her. She needs someone to take care of Sid when she goes into hospital with Fred in just over a week.'

'How long would it be for?' I asked.

'It's hard to know,' Becky told me. 'It depends on how quickly Fred recovers and when he's discharged, but talking to Jo, I would think at least three weeks to a month.

'I wasn't sure, with what was going on at the moment with Nancy, whether you would be up for it,' she told me. 'But I know you're used to juggling and Sid doesn't have any neglect or abandonment issues. It's just a case of giving him somewhere to live while his mum focuses on his brother and his recovery.'

I hadn't looked after a little one in ages and I enjoyed the cuddles, playing with them and reading to them. They were like little sponges at that age, soaking up knowledge about the world around them. I also thought it might be a good distraction for Nancy and bring a bit of fun and silliness to the house, which would be good for both of us.

'OK,' I smiled. 'I'd be happy to help.'

'Brilliant,' smiled Becky. 'Let me talk to Jo and we'll come up with a plan. The operation is in just over a week so I think the best thing to do is for Jo to bring Sid here one afternoon and you can meet her, have a play and get to know him. Then perhaps another night he could come for dinner and then you could pick him up from nursery?'

It was all about him becoming familiar with me and the house so that when he came to stay, he would hopefully settle in quickly.

I was quite excited at the prospect of a new placement. I enjoyed having Nancy here – I liked the challenge, but with Sid being of pre-school age, it meant I could start going to toddler groups and things like that when Nancy was at school, which I hadn't done in ages.

When I picked Nancy up from school, I told her about Sid and explained that he would hopefully be coming to live with us for a little while. I explained that Jo was going to bring Sid round at some point so we could all meet each other.

She looked confused.

'So other children as well as me can live here as well?' she asked.

'Yes, I normally foster two or even three children at a time,' I told her. 'When you came to stay with me, I'd just come back to work after some time off. That's why there was no one else here when you arrived.'

I got some of my old photo albums out and showed her some of the children that I'd looked after over the years.

'Have you looked after anyone else whose mummy killed their daddy?' she asked sadly.

'No, sweetie, I haven't,' I told her. 'I'm just very sad and sorry that it happened to you.'

A few minutes later, my phone rang.

'Hi Maggie, it's DC Hayley Hirst,' said a voice. 'I've just called Juliet too, but I wanted to let you know that Helen Miller appeared in court again this morning. She pleaded guilty to murder and was remanded in custody. There will be a sentence hearing at the crown court in the next few months.'

My heart sank. Any hope of Helen going free had just disappeared and now Nancy was going to have to cope with the fact that her mum was going to be in prison for a very long time.

CHAPTER THIRTEEN

A New Arrival

It wasn't good news but I didn't want to say anything to Nancy that evening until I'd had a chance to talk to Juliet about it. She popped round the following morning and I could see that it was weighing as heavy on her mind as it was on mine.

'What sort of sentence is she facing for murder?' I asked her.

Juliet shrugged.

'I think it depends on what the pre-sentence reports come back with and if there are any mitigating circumstances but murder normally means a life sentence,' she sighed. 'I think it depends on what the judge decides on the day but Hayley said we should prepare ourselves for anything from ten to twelve years at the very least.'

My heart sank. A decade or more. It meant that Nancy would be a fully grown woman before her mother was released from behind bars.

Even though she had shown a lot of anger towards Helen, her mother was also the only person that Nancy had left in the world and I knew this was going to be a huge shock for her.

'What do we do?' I asked Juliet. 'Do we talk to Nancy after the sentencing when we know exactly how long she's got or do we broach it now?'

'I think we need to do it now,' she sighed. 'We have to start preparing her for the fact her mum's going to be locked away for a long time. As we've said all along, we owe it to her to be honest.'

I was dreading telling Nancy as I knew she was going to be devastated but Juliet was keen to do it as soon as possible. When I arrived back home from picking Nancy up from school, Juliet was already waiting outside.

'Hi Nancy,' she smiled as she got out of her car.

'Why is she here?' Nancy whispered to me suspiciously.

Nancy knew enough by now to know that a visit from Juliet normally signified bad news.

'Juliet wanted to pop round to talk to you,' I told her. 'Let's all go inside and I'll put the kettle on.'

We went into the kitchen and sat round the table. Nancy shifted uncomfortably in her seat as she knew instinctively that there was bad news coming. Juliet chatted to her about school but I could see the worried look on her face.

When I'd got everyone a drink, Juliet began to talk.

'I wanted to let you know that DC Hirst got in touch with us,' she told her. 'Your mum went back to court again yesterday and she pleaded guilty to murder. That means she has admitted to stabbing your daddy and killing him.'

It was hard to hear but I admired the fact that Juliet didn't try to dress it up. She just told Nancy the truth which, no matter how harsh, was what she needed to hear.

'Do you understand what that means, Nancy?' I asked her

139

gently. 'If you've got any questions, Juliet and I can try to answer them.'

'But why?' she asked. 'I don't understand. Why did she stab him?'

'Mummy didn't say why, so unfortunately it's very hard for any of us to understand,' I told her.

Juliet began to talk her through what would happen over the next few weeks.

'Your mum will eventually have to go back to court to be sentenced and a judge will decide how she's going to be punished. As you know, taking someone's life is a very, very serious thing to do so you need to be prepared for the fact that the judge will probably send Mummy to prison for a long time.'

Nancy looked at her blankly.

'What's a long time?' she asked her. 'Do you mean a whole year?'

I held my breath, not daring to look at Nancy as I knew her heart would be broken.

'I'm afraid at the very least it could mean that your mum will be in prison for ten years or even twelve,' she told her. 'By the time she's released, you're probably going to be an adult.'

I could see her working it out in her head.

'Ten years?' she gasped. 'But I'll be twenty-one by then. You mean I won't be able to live with Mummy again until I'm a grown-up?'

'I'm afraid it looks that way, sweetie,' I nodded.

Her eyes filled with tears and she looked down at the floor.

'Good,' she said. 'I'm glad. She deserves it. He was the best daddy in the world and she took him away from me.'

Nancy pushed back her chair, got up from the table and walked out of the kitchen.

'I can tell she doesn't mean it,' I sighed.

Even though she was still angry with her mum, I knew this news was devastating for Nancy and she was really going to struggle to accept it. I gave her some time on her own but when Juliet left, I went upstairs to check on her.

She was lying on her bed and I could see by her swollen, red eyes that she'd been crying.

'How are you doing?' I asked her. 'I know that must have been a shock for you.'

'What will happen to me now?' she asked in a small voice. 'If Mummy's in prison for years and years, will I stay with you until I'm an adult?'

'The honest answer is, at this stage I don't know,' I told her. 'That's something that we've all got to talk about over the next few weeks and we need to wait until your mummy goes back to court to be sentenced so we know exactly how long she's likely to be in prison for. I know this is all really hard for you but for now you'll stay here with me and if anything changes then you'll be the first to know.'

I was trying to be as reassuring as I could but I realised that all of this was probably making her feel very insecure and vulnerable.

'How are you feeling about Mummy?' I asked her.

'I'm still cross with her for hurting Daddy and taking him away from us,' she sighed. 'But I'm really sad too that I won't see her for a very long time.'

'I understand why you're feeling cross and sad, sweetie, but you can still see her,' I told her. 'We can arrange for you to go and see her every month at the prison if you wanted to.'

'I'll think about it,' she sighed.

Becky gave me a call that night when Nancy was in bed.

'How did it go today?' she asked me as she'd seen an email from Juliet about Helen.

I explained that Nancy had taken the news badly, which was completely understandable.

'What are you thinking at this stage, Maggie?' she asked me. 'Just so I know going forward. Is taking Nancy on long-term something you'd be interested in doing?'

It would mean that I'd be committing myself to her for the next seven years until she reached eighteen, although I could still take on other placements alongside her.

'I've been thinking about it a lot,' I told her. 'And I'd be happy to foster her for the long-term. She's a lovely girl and I'm already very fond of her.'

I'd only known Nancy a few months but my heart went out to her. She'd been through so much and I cared about her and wanted the best for her.

'Well you don't have to decide now but it's useful for me to know how you're feeling,' Becky told me.

Over the next few days, I kept a close eye on Nancy. She was still going to school every day and she seemed to be coping. I also had Jo and little Sid coming round to meet us and to see the house soon. In a way, it was a welcome distraction for us both.

'Is it tonight that the baby's coming?' she asked me one morning.

'Yes, he'll be here with his mum and brother after school,' I told her. 'He's a toddler, not a baby like Edie though, flower.'

'I know but I bet he's still really cute,' she smiled.

I was also looking forward to meeting them but also slightly nervous about whether Sid would settle with us.

I spent the day sorting out my toy cupboard and making sure that I had lots of things scattered around the house that a three-year-old would like. I got the toy garage down from the loft, as well as some cars, some picture books, Duplo and puzzles.

Nancy and I had just got in from school when there was a knock at the door.

'Do you think that's them?' she asked excitedly as I went to answer it.

I opened the door to find the most adorable little boy standing there. He had curly brown hair and big blue eyes with the longest, darkest eyelashes. As soon as I opened the door, he ran into the hallway.

'Well hello,' I smiled. 'You must be Sid.'

The woman with him laughed. She had shoulder-length brown hair and was pushing an older boy in a specially adapted buggy.

'Hi, I'm Jo,' she said with a strong Polish accent. 'And this is Fred.'

'Come on in,' I smiled.

She explained that Fred was probably better staying in his chair so I helped her wheel it into the kitchen where Sid was already sitting on the floor playing with Nancy.

'Someone's made themselves at home,' I laughed.

I introduced Nancy to everyone and while I made Jo a coffee, Nancy took Sid out into the garden. By now Fred had fallen asleep in his chair and it gave Jo and I a chance to have a chat. She explained how Fred had been born prematurely and it had caused a number of problems including autism, learning difficulties and epilepsy.

The number of seizures he had every day left him exhausted.

'The poor little lad,' I sighed. 'And it must have been so hard for you to cope with on your own.'

Jo nodded and looked a bit teary.

'It is difficult,' she sighed. 'I don't get much sleep and I constantly worry, but I love my boys.'

Fred was going to be having an operation to remove part of his brain in the hope that it would help reduce the number of seizures that he had.

'I feel so guilty about leaving Sid but I just don't a choice,' she sighed. 'Because of all of Fred's other problems, they don't know how long it will take him to recover so we might be in hospital for a while.'

The hospital had arranged for Jo to be able to stay in special family accommodation close to the children's ward.

'Sid will be absolutely fine here with us,' I told her. 'You need to concentrate on Fred and getting him through the surgery.'

'He looks like he's already having the time of his life,' she laughed.

We glanced out of the patio doors to where Nancy was pushing Sid on a swing in the garden and he was giggling away.

'Your daughter's really good with him,' she smiled.

'I'm actually fostering Nancy for a little while,' I explained. 'But yes, she's brilliant with little ones.'

As I'd hoped, it looked like Sid was going to be the perfect distraction for all of us.

Jo talked me through his daily routine and what he liked and didn't like to eat. Eventually he ran in from the garden, so

I took the opportunity to spend a bit of time with him. Nancy and I sat on the floor with him and played Duplo towers. We built them up high then he giggled as he knocked them over.

'Are you going to come and stay with us while Mummy takes your big brother to hospital?' I asked him.

He looked over at Jo and she nodded.

'Yes, we've been talking about it, haven't we, Sid? Mummy's going to be with Fred while the doctors try to make him better and you're going to stay with Maggie.'

'We've got lots of toys for you to play with here,' I told him. 'And as well as the swing, we've got a slide and a sandpit to show you as well.'

'Aren't you lucky, Sid?' smiled Jo. 'Our little flat doesn't have a garden so he'll love all of that.'

He was such a sweet little boy and he seemed very adaptable. Nancy held his hand as she led him upstairs so we could show him his bedroom. I'd fitted a bed guard on the single bed and his duvet cover had planets and rockets on it.

'This is going to be where you go to sleep,' I showed him. 'There are lots of toys and books here too and Nancy's room is just next door. You've even got a special duvet with spaceships on it because Mummy told me that you like space and planets.'

'Where's Mummy and Freddy's room?' he asked.

'Remember Mummy and Fred are going to be sleeping at the hospital,' I gently reminded him.

'Oh yeah,' he grinned. 'I'm a silly billy.'

As far as first meetings go, it couldn't have gone any better. Fred was going into hospital in four days' time so Jo and I had arranged to settle Sid in gradually with us.

'Tomorrow I'm going to pick you up from nursery and bring you back here to have some lunch and a little play,' I told him. 'Then Mummy will collect you later on.'

'She come too?' he asked, pointing to Nancy.

'Nancy's at school tomorrow but you'll see her again another day,' I told him.

Sid's visit had been exactly what Nancy needed and after they'd left, she talked excitedly about how cute he was and how much she was looking forward to him coming to stay with us.

'Can I read him a story, Maggie, and help give him a bath?' she asked me.

'If you want to, lovey, of course you can,' I smiled. 'You're so good with children. Would you have liked to have a little brother or sister of your own?'

Nancy nodded.

'Mummy wanted one too but Daddy wouldn't let us,' she sighed. 'Mummy begged and begged but he said he loved us both too much to share us with anyone else.'

'Oh, that's a shame,' I said.

That evening, as I was getting organised for the following day, I remembered the car was low in petrol. If I was taking Nancy to school and then picking Sid up from nursery, I knew I needed to fill up the tank as there would be no time in the morning.

'Come on,' I told Nancy after dinner. 'Let's pop out to the petrol station. You can choose a chocolate bar if you want.'

'OK,' she sighed reluctantly.

I filled up at the pump while Nancy went into the shop. After much deliberation, she chose a Cornetto instead of a chocolate bar, as it was a warm summer's evening.

'All done,' I said as we got back into the car, pleased that

I was all sorted for the morning. 'Now let's get back.'

'When we get home, don't forget to write it in the book, Maggie,' Nancy told me.

'Book?' I asked her, puzzled. 'What book do you mean?'

'You know, the one like Daddy had. When Mummy put petrol in the car, she wrote it down in his book and showed Daddy the ticket.'

'You mean the receipt?' I asked her and she nodded.

'Did Mummy have to write anything else in the book?' I asked her, both intrigued and alarmed by what I was hearing.

'Oh yes, everything,' she nodded. 'Every time Mummy went in the car, she had to write it down in the book.'

'What kinds of things did she write?'

'She had to put down what time it was when she left the house, where she was going and then what time she got back, as Daddy liked to check it. If she didn't then he got really cross.'

'Why did she have to do that?' I asked her.

'He was always worried about Mummy because he loved her so much and he wanted to know where she had been and how long it had taken her,' she told me. 'Then every night he would check the car and make sure what Mummy had written in the book was true.'

'How did he do that?' I asked, hiding my increasing horror.

She pointed to the milometer on the dashboard and the fuel indicator.

'He always liked to know where Mummy was so he could keep her safe. And Daddy wrote things in the book too,' she added.

'What did Daddy write?' I asked, already dreading what she was going to say.

'Oh, you know, just stuff like how long she was in the toilet for,' she replied. 'He worried about her so much and he wanted to make sure that she was OK.'

My head was spinning. Nancy was telling me this like it was an entirely normal thing to do but I'd never heard anything so weird and controlling. My instincts were telling me that we were starting to build up a picture of how life must have been inside that house. And it wasn't good.

CHAPTER FOURTEEN

Concerns

That night I tossed and turned and I couldn't sleep no matter how hard I tried. I couldn't stop thinking about what Nancy had told me about her dad. It wasn't normal behaviour checking mileage and petrol, writing down where his wife had been and when she'd got back. And timing someone every time they went to the toilet? It was bizarre and very controlling.

All of these things that Nancy had been telling me over the past few weeks had gradually been adding up in my mind and now I was convinced of the fact that something had been very wrong in that house. I couldn't ignore it any longer.

The following morning, after I'd dragged myself out of bed and dropped Nancy off at school, I rang Juliet. I told her about the conversation that Nancy and I had had at the petrol station.

'It's certainly very odd,' she agreed.

'It's not just that; there's been a few things that Nancy has said that have been a bit strange,' I sighed. 'At first I thought they were all just flippant comments but the things she's saying are really starting to ring alarm bells and I don't think we can ignore them any more.'

'Do you think she's making it up?' she asked.

'No, I honestly don't,' I replied. 'She doesn't seem to think there's anything wrong with her dad's behaviour. Her view is that he did these things because he loved her and her mum so much.'

'When you put all of that together, I agree,' she sighed. 'I think I need to talk to DC Hirst and Helen's solicitor and get their opinion.'

Slowly I was learning more about what Nancy and Helen's life had been like at home and I didn't like what I was hearing. It was becoming clear to me that behind closed doors, perhaps Martin wasn't the devoted husband and father everyone had believed him to be.

That afternoon I picked Sid up from nursery and took him back to my house to start helping him settle into my home and his new routine. I made him lunch and we had a play.

'Where's Mummy?' he kept asking and I had to keep reminding him that Mummy was at his house with Fred and they were getting ready to go to the hospital.

'The doctors make Freddy better,' he told me.

'That's right,' I smiled. 'And you're going to stay here with me and Nancy until he's well enough to go home.'

The one thing I'd forgotten about looking after a child this age who was full of energy was that it is exhausting. In amongst all of the mealtimes and the constant snacks, the endless playing and reminding him to go to the toilet, there wasn't much time to think about anything else. But in a way, at this moment in time it was exactly what I needed.

A couple of days later, Sid was due to start his full-time stay with us. Jo thought it would be too upsetting for both of them to bring Sid around herself and then have to say goodbye and leave him, so we decided that she would bring his things around in the morning and I would pick him up from nursery as I'd done a few days ago.

She'd packed some of his favourite books and the scraggy rabbit comforter he'd had since he was a baby.

'I know he's three but he still likes to have a bottle of warm milk at night before he goes to bed,' she told me. 'I know he's too old but he's my baby and I can't help it.'

I could see she was getting teary at the thought of leaving him.

'Don't you worry, he's going to be absolutely fine,' I told her. 'He's going to be spoilt rotten.'

When I went to pick him up from nursery, he seemed confused but happy to be coming back to my house.

'Mummy's gone to hospital with Fred now,' I told him when we got back. 'So you're going to have dinner here and sleep in the bedroom with the space duvet.'

My plan was to keep him entertained and busy all afternoon so that he didn't have time to think about Jo and miss her. I was also keen to tire him out so he slept well that night.

For the next few hours, we didn't stop. We read stories, built Duplo, played in the garden and did painting. Then when Nancy was home, she pushed him on the swing and caught him at the bottom of the slide while I made us all some pasta for tea. Afterwards she helped me give him a bath and get him into his pyjamas. It was only after I'd read him a story and got him his bottle of milk that Sid got a bit teary.

'What is it, petal?' I asked him as he snuggled into my lap on the rocking chair.

'I want Mummy,' he whimpered.

'I know you do but remember Mummy's at the hospital with Fred,' I told him. 'The doctors are going to make his head better. We'll talk to her in the morning though.'

He was very clingy so I lay on the bed with him and cuddled him to sleep. It was lovely to feel his warm little body in my arms as he drifted off.

That evening I texted Jo to reassure her and let her know he'd had a good afternoon and was fast asleep now.

Thankfully he was so shattered, he slept through until 7 a.m. I helped him down the stairs and as he ran into the kitchen, I could see that he was expecting Jo to be there.

Instead there was Nancy, dressed in her school uniform, making breakfast.

'Hello Siddy,' she smiled, making a big fuss of him.

'Where's Mummy?' he asked, looking confused.

'Mummy's going to phone soon,' I told him. 'So you watch my phone and tell me if it rings.'

He was tucking into a bowl of Coco Pops when she called.

'Mummy's on the phone, do you want to say hello?'

'Hello Mummy,' he shouted into the phone. 'I've got chocolate for my breakfast.'

'Ooh that sounds nice darling,' she told him. 'What a treat! What are you going to do today?'

Before he could answer, he'd dropped the phone on the floor and had run off to play with the garage.

'Sorry Jo,' I said, laughing. 'I think you've lost him to the toy cars.'

I could tell she was missing him and was a bit disappointed, but at that age it's impossible to make them chat on the phone.

'It's OK,' she said. 'It sounds like he's having a lovely time.'

'How's Fred?' I asked.

'He had a bit of an unsettled night so we're both shattered,' she said. 'The surgery's booked for tomorrow.'

I could hear the worry in her voice.

'I'll be thinking of you and I hope it goes OK,' I said. 'Sid's absolutely fine, so don't worry. He's settled in really well.'

'Thank you, Maggie,' she said.

Most of the time, Sid was a happy little chap. It was always at night-time that he missed his mum.

I printed out a photo that Jo had emailed me of herself, Sid and Fred and put it by his bed. Every night we gave Mummy and Fred a kiss before he went to sleep.

But at his age, children don't have much of a sense of time and tend to forget things. I bought him some picture books about going into hospital and having an operation to try to give him an understanding about where Fred was. I also picked a teddy out of the toy box and Sid helped me put a bandage on his head.

'This teddy's got a poorly head just like your brother,' I told him. 'What shall we call him?'

'Poo poo,' he giggled in a typical three-year-old fashion.

'Oh no, not poo poo,' I smiled. 'We can't call him that.'

'I call him Fluffy,' he said.

'That's a good idea,' I said. 'Poor Fluffy's got a poorly head but we can look after him and make him better just like Mummy and the doctors are doing with Fred.'

We spent lots of time tucking the teddy into bed and checking his bandage and making sure he was OK and it seemed to help Sid connect with what was happening to his brother.

Thankfully Fred's operation went well, although he had a long recovery ahead of him. After a week, he was more stable and Jo called me to say she was missing Sid desperately.

'If you can leave Fred for an hour, why don't you pick Sid up from nursery and take him to the park?' I suggested.

'Oh, I'd love that,' she told me.

I could tell how much she wanted to see him and it was important for Sid to see her too and understand that she hadn't just disappeared into thin air. It would be too unsettling for him to go back to their flat but a trip to the park and an ice cream with his mummy would be perfect.

Jo dropped him back later that afternoon and when I opened the door, she was carrying Sid in her arms.

'He was so surprised to see me at pick up,' she grinned.

She admitted that she'd been so overwhelmed to see him that she'd cried.

'Where's your teddy, Sid?' she asked him as she put him down. 'Show me the teddy with the special bandage on his head.'

'Have you been telling Mummy all about Fluffy?' I smiled.

He nodded and ran to get him from his bedroom.

'You're right,' she said when he brought him back down. 'Poor Fluffy's got a poorly head just like Fred.'

'Will you look after him if I look after Fred?' she asked him.

'I will, Mummy,' he told her solemnly.

She kissed the teddy.

'Bye bye, Fluffy, get better soon,' she said.

'Mummy's got to go back to the hospital now to see Freddy, sweetie,' I explained.

'See you later, Sid,' smiled Jo, kissing him. 'I love you and I'll see you soon.'

'OK, Mummy,' he said hesitantly.

As I closed the door, there were a few tears. Me, Sid and Fluffy sat on the sofa and had a cuddle.

'Don't you worry,' I soothed. 'When Fred's all better you can go home and live in your house with Mummy again. It's all going to be OK.'

If only I could say the same about Nancy, I told myself as I picked up the phone to Juliet.

CHAPTER FIFTEEN

The Terrible Truth

Settling Sid in had been my focus over the past few days but then Juliet got in touch. She'd spoken to Helen's solicitor, a woman called Amanda Jenkins, who wanted to meet us.

'I've arranged for her to come into Social Services tomorrow morning and I wondered if you could come along too?' she told me.

'What does she want?' I asked.

'I told her about all of the things Nancy has been saying and our concerns, and I think she'd like to talk to us in person about it before she goes to visit Helen in prison.'

I was happy to speak to her if it meant that it would help us to uncover the truth in the long run.

The following morning, after I'd dropped Nancy at school and Sid at nursery, I drove into town to the Social Services' building.

Amanda was already there, waiting in one of the meeting rooms with Juliet, when I arrived. She was in her thirties and smartly dressed in a navy trouser suit.

'Thank you for agreeing to see me,' she said. 'And for passing on all of that information from Nancy. I can see why you were concerned, Maggie.'

'It sounds silly but from the start things didn't add up,' I sighed. 'There have been lots of little comments over the past few months and the more I heard, the more it concerned me.'

'I think you're right to be concerned,' nodded Amanda.

She told us how she had an appointment with Helen at the prison in a couple of days' time.

'Ever since I took Helen on as client, I've tried and tried but I can't seem to get her to talk to me,' she sighed. 'All she will say is the same thing that she's said to the police and the Crown Prosecution Service (CPS) all along, which is that she's responsible for stabbing Martin but she won't say why. Now that she's pleaded guilty, I've told her the kind of sentence that she's facing but even that hasn't got her to open up. From what Nancy has been telling you, and what I think everyone has suspected all along, is that there is a hell of a lot more to this case and I'm determined to get to the bottom of it.'

Amanda explained that she had requested a pre-sentence report. It was an impartial report done by the Probation Service that gives the sentencing judge an idea of a person's background and also helps to give them some understanding as to why that person committed the offence. It was a chance to bring up any extenuating circumstances that might lead to the judge being more lenient and passing a shorter sentence. The court could use the recommendations in the report to decide on the most appropriate sentence for the crime.

'But a report is going to be a complete waste of time if Helen herself is not willing to give anyone any indication about why she committed the crime in the first place,' sighed Amanda.

We'd all met Helen and although I didn't really know her, she didn't strike me as someone who would murder her husband in cold blood for no apparent reason.

'I can see why you're frustrated,' agreed Juliet.

Amanda had a suggestion that she wanted to run past us.

'I'd like you both to come along to the prison with me when I talk to Helen,' she told us. 'I want her to know exactly what Nancy has been saying and I think it would be better coming from you both.'

'It wouldn't normally be something that we'd do,' replied Juliet. 'But if you think it would help then I'd be happy to come along.'

'For Nancy's sake, it's worth a try,' I agreed.

On the morning of the visit, Nancy was at school and Sid was at nursery as usual. I had Louisa on standby to pick him up if for some reason I wasn't back in time.

As Juliet drove us through the gates of the prison, it felt strange being back there again. Amanda was waiting for us outside the entrance and that same feeling of claustrophobia crept over me as I put my belongings into a locker and waited to be searched.

'I don't know what it is about prisons but every time I go into one, I feel really anxious and guilty like I've done some-thing wrong,' sighed Juliet.

'I know exactly what you mean,' I told her.

Again this was deemed as a professional visit so we were allowed to enter the prison outside of the usual allotted visiting times.

Just like before, a prison officer led the three of us into the visiting room where we waited until Helen was brought out. I was shocked when I saw her. She was even thinner than the last time and her face was hollow and pale and she had purple shadows under her eyes. She knew Amanda was coming but she looked surprised to see me and Juliet.

'What's happened?' she asked. 'Is Nancy OK?'

'Nancy's absolutely fine,' Juliet reassured her.

'Helen, I wanted to bring Juliet and Maggie with me today to talk to you about a few things,' Amanda told her.

But Helen's mind was still firmly on her daughter, 'Didn't Nancy want to come and see me?' she asked.

'I'm sorry, but she doesn't want to come at the moment,' I told her. 'She's still very angry and upset about everything that's happened.'

Her eyes filled with tears.

'I understand,' she sniffed. 'Please tell her I love her and that I'm sorry . . . How is she? Is she coping OK?'

'The thing she's struggling with the most, the thing I think we're all struggling with, to be honest, is working out why this happened,' Juliet told her.

'Nancy's very confused – her dad is dead and you're here and none of us can answer her questions or give her an explanation as to why,' I told her gently. 'And that's really hard for a child.'

Helen nodded. A tear rolled down her cheek and she brushed it away with a shaking hand.

'Helen, that's why I wanted to come and see you today,' Amanda told her. 'As you know, in a few weeks' time you're going to be appearing in front of a judge and he or she is going to be sentencing you for murder.'

Helen looked down at the floor and started fiddling with her wedding ring that I noticed she was still wearing.

'As I've explained, murder is perhaps the most serious crime there is and brings with it a mandatory life sentence,' Amanda continued. 'But what "life" means is down to the individual discretion of the judge. You're facing a long, long time in prison, Helen, and it's going to be even longer unless you start talking to us. I brought Maggie and Juliet with me today because Nancy's been saying a few things that have really concerned them.'

Helen suddenly looked up.

'What kind of things?' she asked, looking panicked.

'It was just a few comments at first,' I told her gently. 'Little things that she mentioned that I thought sounded odd. I thought she might have got it wrong, you know how kids do. But then she said some other things and I couldn't ignore any longer.'

'What did she say?' asked Helen desperately, tears filling her eyes again.

Very calmly I went through everything Nancy had said that had been bothering me. I told her some of the comments Nancy had made – how she'd told me how Martin had chosen their clothes, how she wasn't allowed to wear certain things, eat certain foods and that she had to write everything down in a book so Martin knew where she'd been at all times.

As I spoke, Helen sobbed quietly to herself.

'Helen, when Maggie and Juliet told me some of the things Nancy had said, I was shocked,' Amanda told her. 'Because if what she's saying is true, then it sounds like we're starting to get a picture of how things might have been at home for you. And my guess is, it wasn't very nice.'

Helen buried her head in her hands.

'Not very nice?' she blurted out. 'It was a living hell.'

Her voice shook with emotion as she started to speak and she struggled to get the words out.

'For the past twelve years, Martin has controlled my entire life. If you can even call it a life. He decided everything – what I wore, what I ate, what I looked like. I wasn't allowed to wear make-up or perfume when he wasn't around. He bought my clothes for me and every day he chose what I was going to wear.'

'Nancy told me that he chose your clothes because he didn't want you to look like a tart,' I told her, cringing at the word, and Helen's face fell.

'I can't believe that she heard that,' she sighed.

'I think she heard lots of things,' I told her gently.

Amidst her tears she described how she had to tell him where she was at all times.

She explained how, at first, she had thought Martin was the perfect man.

'I was nineteen and had come over to England to be an au pair,' she sighed. 'I was so naïve. It was the first time I'd been away from my family in France. I met Martin in a bar and he seemed like the perfect Englishman – he was polite and charming and gave me so many compliments.'

Helen explained that within a year they were married and Martin had forced her to be dependent on him for everything.

'My family weren't happy because it was so quick but I was madly in love,' she smiled sadly. 'But I should have seen the signs.'

Martin had convinced her to give up her job and, rather than get married in France as she had wanted, they'd eloped to Gretna Green.

'He told me his parents were dead and he didn't have any family,' she sighed. 'And he didn't seem to have any friends outside of work acquaintances, which is odd for someone in their thirties. It was all very subtle at first. He told me he wanted to spend every minute with me and he got jealous if I arranged to meet friends. He kicked up a fuss about me going back to France to see my family so I cancelled the trip.'

Helen described how when she had Nancy, she thought things would be different.

'I loved being a mum and Martin was a great dad,' she sighed. 'He was devoted to Nancy but nothing I did was right. I struggled to breastfeed and he told me I was a failure, I wasn't dressing her right, feeding her well enough, not getting her into a routine. It was exhausting. I really wanted to have another baby but Martin wouldn't let me,' she sighed. 'He'd hand me my contraceptive pill every morning and watch while I took it.'

I couldn't imagine how awful it must have been living with someone who treated me like that.

Helen described how, over the years, things had gradually got worse. Before she'd realised what was happening, Martin had made her totally dependent on him.

'I wasn't allowed to have a mobile phone, bank cards or any money of my own; I had to ask him for everything, to beg for every single penny.

'Nancy was right about the book. I had to clock in and clock out like I worked in a factory. I had to write down where I'd been, how long I'd been gone for. Every night Martin checked the mileage on the car against what I'd written in the book and if he didn't think it added up or if he thought I was lying then I'd be punished.'

'Did he ever hit you?' asked Amanda.

'No,' she shook her head. 'He was never ever violent. In a terrible way, I wish he had been. Then I'd have proof, a reason, something to show someone to prove how he treated me.'

'How did he punish you?' asked Amanda.

Helen paused and looked away.

'He'd force himself on me,' she whispered. 'You know, sexually.'

'Oh Helen, I'm sorry,' I said.

'Or he'd destroy something that he knew was precious to me or held special memories,' she continued. 'Like a necklace that belonged to my late grandmother, old family photos or the sleep suit I brought Nancy home from the hospital in. Or sometimes, when he ran out of things to get rid of, he'd make me stand outside for hours on end, sometimes in the freezing cold or the snow and the rain. Thankfully it was always when Nancy was in bed but I'd have to stand there like a statue in the dark for hours on end until he decided I could come in.'

I thought back to what the neighbour Eleanor had said about looking out of the window and seeing Helen standing in the garden in the driving rain and suddenly it all made sense.

'Most of it was psychological,' she sighed. 'Pure mental torture.'

'Why didn't you tell anyone or say anything?' asked Amanda.

'Who would I tell?' she shrugged. 'Martin had alienated me from everyone. I'd lost touch with my family, I wasn't allowed to have any friends or see anyone or go anywhere. The only times I went out were to take Nancy to school or go to the shops. Even if I had, who would believe me? From the outside looking in, I had the perfect life – a husband with a successful business so I didn't need to work. Nice cars, a big house, a daughter in private school, holidays. But behind closed doors, it was absolute hell.'

I think we were all guilty of thinking that way. When I thought of someone being abused by their partner, I would think of the tell-tale signs like the broken ribs and the black eyes and children acting out at school. Emotional abuse was harder to spot and pinpoint.

'When you're in it, it's so hard to get out of it. Martin made me feel like it was me, that everything was my fault. I was fat, a useless wife and mother whose family wanted nothing to do with me. It's only coming here, to this place, listening to other women, that I've started to realise that maybe it wasn't me. Maybe it wasn't my fault.'

She described how for the past few years she'd kept a diary and written everything down in it.

'How come the police didn't find it?' asked Juliet.

'I made sure that I hid it somewhere no one would ever find it,' she told us. 'I didn't want to risk Martin seeing it.'

She described how it was pushed under a floorboard, under the carpet in Nancy's bedroom.

'And what about the book you had to write in for Martin?' asked Amanda, making a note.

'I'm not sure, but I think Martin kept it in some work files in his study,' she said.

Then Amanda asked the question that we were all desperate to know the answer to.

'I know this must be so hard for you to talk about, Helen, but what happened that night?' she asked. 'The night Martin died.'

Helen took a deep breath.

'It wasn't just about me any more,' she sighed. 'As Nancy got older and wanted to be more independent, I could see Martin wanted to control her too. She wasn't allowed to have people round after school or see friends or do anything really. I was scared for her. Scared that she was going to end up like me and not be allowed to have a life.'

Helen explained that for the past few years, she'd been saving up money so that she could leave him.

'I couldn't get away with much, otherwise Martin would notice,' she told us. 'So it was just a few pounds here and there but it started to add up.'

'Was that the money hidden in the toy penguin?' I asked.

'Yes,' she nodded. 'Did Nancy tell you that?'

'She noticed it was gone,' I nodded.

'All I needed was a couple of hundred pounds – enough money for two ferry tickets for Nancy and me. My plan was to get to my parents in France and then I knew I'd be safe. But that day he'd found it.'

She explained that somehow Martin had known about the money hidden in the penguin.

'I know Nancy didn't tell him because I'd told her it was a surprise and I was saving up to buy a present for her dad,' she said. 'I thought I was getting paranoid but for a while I was convinced that he'd hidden cameras around the house so he could spy on me when he was at work. There were things he seemed to know about my day that he couldn't have known unless he was keeping tabs on me. All I can think is there must have been one in Nancy's bedroom because that night he told me that he knew about the money in the penguin.'

Helen explained that she'd told Martin that she was going to leave him.

'Do you know what he did? He just laughed. He laughed in my face. He told me I was never going to leave him. No one else would ever want me and he had taken the money. I was just so upset,' she sobbed. 'All those months and years of saving. That was mine and Nancy's escape route and now we were stuck. I couldn't bear it. I couldn't bear for her to grow up like that.'

Helen could barely get the words out as she described how as she'd turned to walk away, Martin had grabbed her by the hair and pulled her back.

'My eyes were watering from the pain,' she sighed. 'And he told me that if we ever left him then he would find us and he would kill us both. And I believed him, I really did. If he couldn't control us any more then I truly believed that's what he would do.'

Helen was shaking so much now that she could barely talk. 'I was so, so scared,' she sobbed. 'I'd never seen him like that before, that angry and out of control. He pushed me against the work surface and I thought he was going to rape me. Then my hand felt the knife block next to me. It all happened so fast. I don't even remember doing it but as he was about to pin me down, I grabbed a knife and pushed it into his side. I killed him,' she sobbed. 'I picked up the knife and I stabbed him.'

CHAPTER SIXTEEN

Difficult Conversations

It broke my heart to think of what Helen had had to endure and how much pain she must be in. I couldn't just sit there and watch her get more and more distressed – I had to do something.

I got up off my chair, crouched down on the floor next to her and put my arms around her. She felt so frail, I could feel her spine sticking out from under her grey prison sweatshirt, and she was trembling.

'It's OK,' I soothed. 'Thank you for telling us the truth.'

Normally, you weren't allowed to get up off your seat and go over to a prisoner during a visit. But I saw Juliet glance over at the officer sitting in the corner watching us. Thankfully she gave her a nod back to say it was fine.

It took a long time for Helen to catch her breath and start to calm down. Eventually the tears stopped and I walked back to my chair.

'I'm so sorry,' she sighed, trying to compose herself. 'I've never ever talked to anyone about this before or said it out loud and I'm finding it really hard.'

'I can understand,' I told her, smiling sympathetically.

'Helen, why didn't you tell the police any of this when you were being interviewed?' asked Amanda.

'Because who would believe me?' she shrugged. 'Martin had never hit me. I didn't have any cuts or bruises or scars that I could show them. He'd pulled my hair but I didn't have any marks on my body that proved it was self-defence and I'd never called the police or told anyone. He didn't drink or gamble. To the outside world, he was the perfect husband and father and I had just killed him.'

She explained that she was also in deep shock.

'I couldn't actually believe what I'd done myself,' she sighed. 'It didn't seem real. It still doesn't. Every morning when I wake up here, I can't believe that it's happened and that I did that. It all feels like an horrendous dream.'

She started to get teary again.

'And I didn't say anything because I didn't want to make excuses,' she sobbed. 'I deserve to be punished. I took a man's life and I took Nancy's dad away from her and I'll never, ever forgive myself for that as long as I live. And the worst thing is, despite all of this, part of me still loves Martin. That's how messed up all of this is.'

Tears streamed down her face and my heart went out to her. Of course I could never justify killing someone but I couldn't imagine what it must have been like for her being treated like that, being under someone's control for so many years.

'What will happen now?' she asked in a quiet voice. 'Please don't tell Nancy any of this. I'm begging you.'

I looked at Juliet and I knew we were both thinking the same thing.

'Helen, I think Nancy deserves to know,' Juliet told her. 'At the moment she's finding it hard to accept things and can't start to move on. This will be difficult for her to hear but at least she might start to understand why.'

'But what will you tell her?' sobbed Helen. 'How will you explain it to her?'

'I don't think *we* should tell her anything,' replied Juliet. 'I think it needs to come from you.'

Helen's face crumpled.

'I can't do that,' she panicked. 'She worshipped her dad. How do you explain that to a child? What do I say?'

I knew it would be difficult for her but I completely agreed with Juliet. I felt that Helen was the one who needed to tell Nancy the truth. She owed her that much.

'I think you've just got to be honest with her like you've been with us today,' Juliet explained. 'And she might be angry and upset, but in time, as she gets older, she might start to understand it.'

'I don't think I can,' sighed Helen.

'It's really important for Nancy to hear it from you and to know that how Martin treated you wasn't right,' I added. 'She saw a lot of how he treated you and he controlled her too. How would you feel if she went through life thinking that's how relationships work?'

'I couldn't bear it,' sighed Helen. 'I don't ever want that kind of life for her.'

The prison officer came walking over to us.

'I'm afraid this visit's over now and I need to take her back to the cells,' she told us.

Helen stood up.

'OK,' she nodded, before she walked away. 'I'll talk to Nancy. I'll tell her the truth.'

'Thank you,' Juliet said.

Helen looked exhausted and I knew the visit had been emotional and draining for her.

'I know this must have been hard for you but I'll give you a call tomorrow and we can have a chat then,' Amanda told her.

'Thank you for being so open with us,' said Juliet. 'I'll arrange with the prison to bring Nancy to see you in a few days.'

'OK, thank you,' Helen nodded.

'Hopefully I'll see you soon with Nancy,' I told her.

As she was led through the doors by two prison officers, I felt a great deal of sadness but also a sense relief. I hoped that now we had all of this new information, it would have an impact on her case. Emotional abuse was just as devastating and horrific as physical abuse but I knew it was also very difficult to prove.

On our way out, Amanda stopped to speak to the prison officer.

'That was a really hard visit for Helen and as you could probably see, she was quite upset. I'd be really grateful if someone could check on her later to make sure she's OK.'

'We will,' she nodded.

The three of us stood in the visitor's car park and had a chat before we all went in our different directions.

'Gosh that was hard to hear,' sighed Juliet. 'That poor woman.'

'It's horrific,' I agreed.

'What will happen now?' I asked Amanda.

'I'll get in touch with the police and the Crown Prosecution Service (CPS) and let them know that I believe there's new evidence in the case,' she told us. 'Hopefully they'll agree.

They might want to take a new statement from Helen and perhaps Nancy too.'

'Do you think it will help get her a shorter prison sentence?' I asked. .

'There are no guarantees,' she shrugged. 'My argument will be as new evidence has come to light, I'll be appealing to the Crown to reduce the charges from murder to manslaughter.'

'Can they do that when someone has already pleaded guilty?' asked Juliet.

'It's certainly not common practice but it's not impossible,' she told us. 'I think it would help if we could find Helen's diary and the book she was talking about where Martin logged all of her movements.'

Juliet explained that Martin's friend, Dominic, currently had the key for the house but that he could arrange for Amanda or one of her work colleagues to go in.

I got back in time to pick Sid up from nursery, I felt exhausted. I knew that when I picked Nancy up from school school, I couldn't mention anything to her about going to see Helen and what she'd said. Juliet and I needed to have that conversation with her about going to see her mum in prison. Nancy was still very angry with her so there was a chance she might even refuse to go.

Juliet called me early the following morning to let me know that the police did want to take a new statement from Nancy. DC Hirst was going to do it at the same police station as before.

'They want to interview her as soon as possible, Maggie, and before she goes to visit Helen in prison so Helen can't be accused of priming her in any way about what to say,' she told me.

'What do I tell Nancy though?' I asked.

'Just explain that Hayley wants to check a few things with her before her mum goes back to court.'

Thankfully Nancy didn't question it when I told her.

'Flower, you need to go to the police station to see Hayley after school today,' I told her. 'Juliet will pick you up.'

I explained that I had to stay at home to look after Sid and she seemed fine with that.

When she got back, she seemed OK too.

'How did that go?' I asked her.

She shrugged.

'She just asked me lots of questions about Daddy and Mummy and what happened at home,' she told me. 'I answered them all.'

While Nancy went into the house to see Sid, I managed to grab a quiet word with Juliet outside.

'She handled that really well,' she told me. 'Hayley chatted to her and she pretty much told her all of the things that you had mentioned to me. It backs up everything that Helen told us yesterday.'

'Good,' I nodded.

Juliet explained that she was going to leave it a few days as she didn't want to bombard Nancy and she wanted Helen to have a bit of breathing space. But then she would talk to Nancy about going to visit her mum in prison.

I was dreading the conversation, as I had no idea how Nancy was going to react but a couple of days later, Juliet came round and we bit the bullet.

'Juliet has got something really important that she wants to talk to you about,' I told her.

She explained that Helen's solicitor had been to see her in prison.

'Your mum has made a new statement to the police that's given them a bit more of an understanding about why she hurt Daddy.'

'Why? What did she say?' she asked curiously.

'Your mummy really wants to talk to you, lovey, and tell you herself,' I explained. 'So she'd like you to go to the prison again and see her.'

'But she killed my daddy,' she sighed, 'and I don't want to see her or go back to that horrible place.'

'Mummy knows that she did a terrible thing but she wants to try to explain it to you and answer some of your questions.'

'But why can't you tell me?' she sighed.

'We think you really need to hear it from your mum,' said Juliet.

'Can Maggie come with me?' she asked.

'I'm sure that won't be a problem,' I reassured her. 'We can go one morning when Sid's at nursery.'

'OK then,' she sighed. 'But I might not want to listen.'

Sometimes I think as adults we talk to children too much. I could see that Nancy was fed up and exhausted with all the talking and she just needed to be left alone for a few days and have the chance to be an eleven-year-old child again. It was the weekend and we were due to go and see Helen in prison on Monday morning but I was determined we weren't going to spend the next few days going on about it. I let Nancy know that I was happy to answer any of her questions and worries if she had any, but that I wasn't going to bring it up unless she wanted me to.

Instead, we spent our time just being silly and having fun with Sid. We did some finger painting, played in the sandpit with him and took him to the park. Jo texted or rang me every day to see how he was doing. Unfortunately, Fred had suffered a few complications after his operation.

'Sid asks about you and Fred every day and he kisses your photo before he goes to sleep,' I told her.

'Bless him,' she sighed. 'I miss him so much.'

'I know you do,' I told her. 'But Sid is fine so you focus on getting Fred better.'

On Saturday night, Louisa dropped Edie round to us. We were babysitting for her while she went out for a meal with Charlie. It was the first time that they'd been out together at night since she was born and I could see Louisa was nervous but excited.

'Charlie's leaving work so I'm going to meet him at the pub,' she told me, handing me a changing bag. 'Ring me if you need anything or if she won't settle.'

'You go and enjoy yourselves, she's going to be absolutely fine,' I smiled.

I got Edie out of her pram while Nancy watched curiously as Louisa brushed her hair in the hallway mirror and got a lipstick out of her bag and put some on.

'Won't Charlie get really cross when he sees you wearing that?' Nancy asked her.

'What do you mean, sweetie?' replied Louisa, puzzled.

'You're putting lipstick on and he hasn't given you permission,' Nancy told her.

Louisa burst out laughing.

'I don't need Charlie's permission to put lipstick on,' she smiled.

Nancy looked confused and when Louisa had gone, I had a chat to her about it.

'Did your mummy wear lipstick?' I asked her.

'Only when she was with Daddy and he said she could,' she told me. 'And if she didn't ask him, then he'd know when he did the measuring and he would be really cross.'

'The measuring?' I asked curiously.

'Yes, you know, at night Daddy would measure Mummy's lipstick and perfume to make sure she hadn't been using them without asking him,' she told me. 'You don't have a husband, Maggie, so you don't know but it's something husbands do when they love you very much.'

'Oh, I see,' I nodded, trying to hide my shock.

She was so matter-of-fact about it and as far as Nancy was concerned, this sort of behaviour was normal life. She'd grown up in this controlling environment and I knew it was going to take a long time for her to understand that this wasn't how people should treat each other.

As Monday morning came round, my stomach churned with nerves. I really wanted Nancy to go and see her mum and hear what she had to say. But I also knew that if Nancy changed her mind and suddenly decided she didn't want to go then we couldn't make her.

Once again, Sid was a great distraction as we had to drop him off at nursery first. Nancy sat in the back with him making him laugh and she held his hand as he skipped up to the nursery door.

When we got back in the car and it was just the two of us, Nancy was very quiet.

'I don't see why Mummy's making me come and see her again,' she sighed.

'Just give her a chance and hear what she's got to say, poppet,' I told her.

I don't think anyone ever enjoys going to visit someone in prison but at least this time she knew exactly what to expect. Juliet was waiting for us in the car park so we could go through the security checks together.

This time, though, Helen was already waiting for us in the visiting room and I could see that that had thrown Nancy.

As we walked towards her, Helen started to cry as she saw her daughter.

'Oh Nancy, my love, it's so good to see you. 'I've missed you so, so much,' she sobbed. 'I'm sure you've got even taller. Maggie must be feeding you well.'

Nancy didn't say a word or go over to her. She sat down on one of the plastic chairs opposite her mother with her arms folded defensively.

'I'm really glad you've come because I wanted to talk to you about something really important,' Helen told her nervously.

As she began to speak, I took a deep breath – I knew this was going to be very hard for both her and Nancy.

'I know you're grieving for Daddy and you're still very angry at me and I understand that,' she told her. 'But I wanted to explain to you what things were like for me at home with Daddy.'

Nancy looked down at the floor and started kicking her feet against the legs of her chair. She was doing her best to look disinterested.

I could see how upset and nervous Helen already was but I was willing her to get through this.

'Your daddy didn't treat me very well and he did some not very nice things that made me feel very sad,' she told her.

Nancy looked up.

'No, he didn't,' she snapped. 'He loved us so much and he'd do anything for us.'

'Nancy, I know this is hard for you to understand but Daddy liked both of us to be dependent on him. He wanted to control us.'

She tried to explain that it wasn't normal for people who were married to tell each other what they could or couldn't do.

'Daddy decided everything,' she continued. 'Remember how he picked our clothes every day and he chose what we ate and when we ate it? I wasn't allowed to wear make-up and perfume unless he said so or have any money of my own and I had to write down in Daddy's book where I'd been and how long I'd been there. I wasn't allowed to see my family, have any friends or go anywhere without him.'

'Yes, but Daddy did all that because he loved you so much,' she told her. 'And he wanted you to be safe.'

'People who love you don't control you and tell you what to do every minute of every day,' Helen urged, as she started to cry.

'I was so unhappy,' she sighed. 'I couldn't breathe in that house. I couldn't be myself. We weren't allowed to do anything unless Daddy said so. I could never take you to the park, or take you to do something fun, or make friends with the other parents at school because of how angry he would get. You know that Daddy was only happy when we were both at home with him.'

'But Daddy wasn't a bad man,' Nancy replied angrily. 'You're lying. He was a nice man and he loved us and did everything for us. Remember, we'd be nothing without him.'

'That's what he'd always tell us, Nancy, but it was another way of him controlling us,' she sighed.

It was such a hard thing for an eleven-year-old to get their head around.

'And Daddy was starting to control you too,' she told her. 'Remember how you weren't allowed to meet friends or go to their houses after school or invite them round to our house? Remember how Daddy chose your clothes too and what you ate if we ever went out?'

'But I didn't mind,' nodded Nancy.

'But as you got older, I wanted you to be able to do lots of things and go to different places and not have to be told what to do and lead the same sort of miserable life that I was living.'

Nancy shook her head.

'But even if he was mean to you sometimes, he didn't deserve to die,' she snapped. 'You shouldn't have killed him. You're the bad person, not him.'

'I never intended for that to happen,' Helen pleaded. 'I will never, ever forgive myself for taking your daddy's life and I'm so, so sorry for that. What I did was very wrong but how we lived was wrong too.'

She took a deep intake of breath.

'I don't ever expect you to forgive me but I hope that one day you might understand why I hurt Daddy.'

Nancy looked sad rather than annoyed now.

'But why did you do it?' she asked. 'Why did you stab him?'

'Daddy found out that I didn't want to live with him any more,' she told her. 'Remember that money I hid in your cuddly penguin?'

Nancy nodded.

'It wasn't for a present for Daddy like I told you. I'd been saving up for a very long time so I could pay for ferry tickets for you and I to get to France.'

'But why were we going to go to France?' Nancy asked, confused.

'Because I desperately wanted to see my family,' she sighed. 'Daddy cut me off from them and wouldn't let me see them. But I missed my parents so much and I wanted them to meet you. I knew if we could just get there, we'd be safe and we could have a new life and be happy.'

She paused.

'But somehow Daddy found that money in the penguin and he took it. And I was so, so sad because that was my only chance to get away. I couldn't live like that any more. 'Daddy was very angry when I told him I wanted to leave and he said some things that made me very, very scared. It all happened so quickly and before I knew what I was doing I'd grabbed the knife and . . .'

Her voice trailed off and she couldn't get the words out as she started to sob hysterically.

'I'm so sorry, Nancy,' she whispered. 'I really, really am.'

Nancy was crying now too. I put my arm around her shoulders but she shrugged me off.

She got up off her chair, ran over to Helen and threw her arms around her.

'It's OK, Mummy, don't cry,' she soothed. 'We can just tell the judge that you didn't mean it and you can come home and we can live together again. It will be OK, I promise.'

The pair of them sobbed in each other's arms while I wished with all my heart that that could be true.

CHAPTER SEVENTEEN

A Family Reunion

Tears streamed down Helen's face as she savoured every minute of hugging her daughter. Eventually they pulled apart and she smoothed down Nancy's hair.

'Now Mummy's told the truth and said she's sorry, can she come home with us?' Nancy asked Juliet.

'Unfortunately, Nancy, I don't think it's as simple as that,' she told her.

'I'll still have to go back to court, darling, and see a judge,' Helen told her.

'And will they still send you to prison?' Nancy asked.

'I think they will,' nodded Helen. 'They have to. What I did was wrong and I need to be punished.'

By the end of the visit, I could see Helen was exhausted. I knew it must have taken a lot of courage to talk to Nancy so honestly and openly. I hoped that it was also a massive relief for her. Part of me was also thankful that she had purposely left out some of the more upsetting details such as Martin threatening to kill them both or the times in the past that he'd forced her to have sex with him. Maybe they were things that she'd talk to Nancy about in the future as she got older but for now, she didn't want to add to her trauma.

'Will you come and see me again another time?' Helen asked Nancy as she hugged her goodbye.

'Yes, if I'm allowed to,' she replied.

'We can definitely arrange that, Nancy,' Juliet reassured her.

Helen looked very tearful again as she was led off by a prison officer.

As we walked out to the main entrance, we chatted to Nancy.

'How did it feel seeing Mummy today?' I asked her.

'I was really angry at her and I didn't think I wanted to listen to what she was saying,' she sighed. 'But when I saw her, I stopped being cross and I realised that I missed her a lot.'

Nancy started to cry and I stopped in the corridor to give her a cuddle.

'I know you do,' I told her. 'And I can tell Mummy misses you a lot too.'

I held her hand as we walked outside.

'I'm so glad that you decided to come and visit your mummy today,' I said. 'It must have been really hard for you to hear the things that she was telling you but I'm pleased that you gave her a chance.'

'I didn't know that she felt so sad and that Daddy made her unhappy,' she sighed.

'It's not your fault,' I soothed. 'You're a child. It's not your job to know if your parents are happy or not.'

I knew it would take her a long time to process what had happened and she probably wouldn't fully understand it until she was an adult and had her own relationships.

What I was worried about was that she still seemed to think that now Helen had told everyone the truth, she was going to be able to come home.

'Your mum's solicitor is going to talk to the judge and explain how unhappy she was and why Mummy did this but that still doesn't make what she's done OK,' Maggie told Nancy.

'Do you think she will still go to prison?' she asked and I nodded.

'Mummy's still done something wrong and needs to be punished. But hopefully the judge will understand how sad and worried she was feeling so she might not have to go to prison for as long. But there are no guarantees.'

We said goodbye to Juliet and headed home.

'I know this is a lot of information for you to absorb and over the next few days you might think of lots more questions,' I said in the car on the way home.

'If it helps, what you can do is ask me or write them down, and Juliet and I will try to answer them or we can send them to Mummy and she can write back to you.'

She nodded. I could see she was shell-shocked and struggling to take everything in.

All I could do was help her try to make sense of things and slowly try to teach her how normal adult relationships worked and understand that the way her dad had behaved wasn't right.

That night I emailed Becky to let her know how the visit to the prison had gone. I also called my friend Vicky for a chat. She was a fellow foster carer so I knew that I could speak to her in confidence. It had been an emotionally charged day and it always helped me to process things when I could talk to somebody else about it.

'Wow,' sighed Vicky when I told her what had been going on and about today's prison visit. 'That's a lot for a child to get their head around and understand.'

'She's grown up in that environment so she doesn't know any different,' I replied.

'I think emotional abuse is hard sometimes even for adults to understand,' said Vicky.

That was my big worry. It was difficult to prove and I hoped the judge who sentenced Helen would see the truth.

'When you talk to Helen, you can see she's a broken woman,' I sighed. 'She's lived with that constant belittling for such a long time. It sounds as though it was a constant grinding down, with Martin telling her that she was no good, that nothing she did was right. I think that she'd started to believe it.'

Helen had no self-esteem and she didn't think she was worthy of anything.

'It's so sad,' sighed Vicky. 'I can't imagine being controlled by someone for all those years.'

I could see that Nancy was trying to get her head around it all too. She was tucking into breakfast one morning when she started chatting about Charlie and Louisa.

'Remember the other day,' she said, 'when I asked Louisa if Charlie had given her permission to wear lipstick and she laughed?'

'That's right,' I nodded. 'Louisa thought it was funny because she doesn't need Charlie's permission to do anything. If she wants to wear lipstick or wear a dress that she likes, she can do it.'

'So she chooses all her own clothes?' asked Nancy.

'Yes,' I nodded. 'She buys her own clothes and she wears exactly what she wants to wear and Charlie does too. He doesn't control Louisa and they decide on things together.'

I could see her slowly taking in what her mum had told her and trying to get it clear in her mind but she was only eleven and it would be a few years until she really understood what had happened at home.

I wanted to teach her that it was OK for her to make her own choices, something she had found really difficult when she had first come to live with me. So I'd encourage her to choose her own clothes at the weekend and pick what she'd like us to have for dinner. It was important to give her confidence in her own opinions.

Early the following week, Juliet called me. Behind the scenes, she had been talking to Helen's parents, Claude and Marie, in France. They hadn't seen their daughter for twelve years.

'They're obviously very shocked and upset by what's happened and they're worried sick for Helen,' she told me.

She explained that a couple of days ago, they'd come over from France and yesterday they'd been to see Helen in prison.

'How did it go?' I asked.

'After all that time I think it was very emotional,' she sighed. 'Helen told them everything that had been going on at home and they're devastated.'

They were planning to stay in the UK for the next few weeks and were staying at Nancy's old house.

'They want to talk to Helen's solicitor and visit her in prison as often as they can,' she told me. 'They're also very keen to meet Nancy.'

'I can imagine,' I said.

Even though they were her grandparents, they were strangers to Nancy so it was important to meet them somewhere neutral. We wanted everyone to be as relaxed as possible and for it to be informal, so Juliet and I agreed that it would be better happening at a park rather than in a meeting room at Social Services. When I told Nancy about it, she seemed excited.

'I'd like to see them,' she nodded. 'I haven't had grand-parents before and Mummy talked about them to me lots in secret, when Daddy wasn't listening.'

I explained that we were going to meet them at the weekend in the local park.

'But how will we know who they are?' she asked.

'Don't worry, Juliet is going to be there so she can intro-duce us all,' I told her.

We'd arranged to meet at the café in the park, which was right next to a playground. It meant we could all sit and chat, but if things got too much then Nancy could go off and play if she wanted to. I also had Sid with me and as a wriggly three-year-old, I knew he wouldn't sit still for long but Juliet said she would help keep him occupied.

I could tell Nancy was nervous as we walked through the park towards the café. Juliet had texted me to say they were sitting on the wooden benches outside.

'What if they don't like me?' she worried.

'Of course they will, sweetie,' I smiled. 'What's not to like? You're a lovely girl.'

She looked anxiously around.

'I can't see them,' she worried. 'I don't think they've come.'

Then I saw Juliet waving at me in the distance.

'There they are,' I said, waving back.

I'd been expecting an elderly couple, but Claude and Marie were a sprightly pair in their mid-fifties, which reinforced how young Helen had been when she'd met Martin. They were both grey-haired, but tanned and athletic and wore T-shirts, shorts and trainers that made them look like they were keen walkers. Neither of them could take their eyes off Nancy as we walked towards the picnic bench where they were sitting.

'Nancy, this is your granny and grandpa,' Juliet said.

They couldn't wipe the smiles off their faces as Juliet introduced them.

'Hello,' said Nancy shyly.

I could see Marie was doing her best to hold back the tears.

'Oh, you look just like your mama did when she was a girl,' she gasped. 'You've got Claude's brown eyes and the same lovely long hair as Helen.'

My French was very rusty so I was relieved to hear Marie speaking impeccable English.

'Hello Nancy,' smiled Claude, also speaking in English. 'We've been so looking forward to meeting you. Your mama told us all about you.'

'Oh, you've seen Mummy?' she asked.

'Yes,' nodded Claude. 'We went to visit her yesterday.'

Sometimes, even though family members haven't met each other before, there's an immediate bond or connection. Perhaps it's genetics or a familiarity in their looks or mannerisms, but Nancy seemed instantly comfortable with her grandparents. They happily chatted away as Juliet, Sid and I went to get us all some drinks.

'They're a really lovely couple,' I smiled, lifting Sid up so he could choose a juice from the cabinet. 'And Nancy seems happy.'

Juliet offered to take Sid to the playground while I sat with Nancy and her grandparents. I took the drinks back to the table and they were still talking.

As I handed Nancy her hot chocolate and gave Marie and Claude their coffee, they were telling her all about where they lived in the south of France.

'Why didn't you ever come and see me?' she asked them sadly.

'We didn't know you existed, my darling,' Marie told her. 'We haven't seen your mother for many years. Your father didn't like your mama having contact with us. We rang her every week at first, but he always said that she wasn't at home or when we did get hold of her, she would barely speak to us. We wrote and sent birthday cards but then one day they got returned to us and it said that your mama no longer lived at that address.'

'Oh, I saw some of the cards that you sent her,' nodded Nancy. 'Mummy showed them to me and she told me all about you.'

'Oh, she kept them?' asked Marie, sounding surprised.

'Yes, she had them in a special box,' Nancy nodded. 'But she hid them from Daddy because she said he'd be cross if he saw them.'

I was keen to move the conversation away from Martin so I quickly changed the subject.

'What sort of things did your mum tell you about Granny and Grandpa then, Nancy?' I asked.

'She told me lots of things,' she replied. 'How she used to pick the blackberries and make jam with you. And how you would go to the beach in the summer and jump in the waves.'

Marie's eyes filled with tears.

'Ah, she remembered,' she smiled. 'Yes, your mummy loved making jam although she was far better at the tasting than the making.'

'Remember that time she got it all down her dress and she was a sticky mess?' laughed Claude. 'Your granny was very cross.'

'I like jam too,' smiled Nancy.

'Well maybe we could teach you how to make it?' suggested Marie. 'I'd like that very much.'

But I could see the tears in her eyes and I guessed that she was thinking about all those years they'd missed seeing their grandchild grow up.

Claude, sensing his wife's upset, reached over the table and gave her hand a squeeze.

'So, Nancy, are you any good at climbing?' he asked her, glancing at the climbing frame.

'I don't know,' she said. 'I never really went to playgrounds before I lived at Maggie's house.'

'Well, why don't you and I go to the climbing frame over there and you can see if you can beat me to the top.'

'OK,' she laughed. 'But I think I probably will.'

As they walked off together, Marie smiled.

'He always wanted to be a grandpa,' she sighed. 'We've got so many lost years to make up for.'

'It must have been so hard for you losing touch with Helen,' I said, and she nodded.

'She was our only child,' she sighed. 'It was so devastating for us when we lost contact with her. We felt so powerless, and we missed her so much. But as soon as she met Martin, we lost her. No matter what we did, we just didn't seem to be able to reach her.'

She told me how Helen had come over to England as an impressionable teenager. Within months, she'd met Martin and fallen in love.

'I think from the beginning, he didn't want to share her with anyone else,' she sighed. 'She always made excuses why she couldn't come back to France for holidays.

'We came over to the UK a few times but he would never come and meet us. I think we saw him twice and he was rude and hardly said a word. We so wanted to get to know him, but he just wasn't interested. We were terrified that if we said anything negative about him to Helen, then we'd lose her altogether.'

She described how it was a huge shock to hear that they'd run away and got married on their own after a few months.

'Helen had always dreamed of a big fairy-tale wedding, so it was such a surprise when we learned that they'd eloped without even telling us. But she was nineteen and there was nothing we could do to stop her. We tried to let her know we were there for her – we'd always been so close in the past, but slowly we could feel her pulling away from us,' she sighed. 'The phone calls home went from once a week to once a month.

'She was always busy and never seemed to have time to talk, even though she told us she'd given up work. We tried writing to her but we never got a reply.'

Then their letters and cards were returned to them saying that she no longer lived at that address.

'We were so worried,' she sighed. 'The number we had didn't work any more, we didn't have their new address. We knew Martin had his own company and eventually we found out that number and called him at work. He was so cold and dismissive on the phone. He told us that Helen didn't want to be in touch with us any more and that she had a new life now in the UK. Then we got a letter from her saying the same thing. It was her handwriting so we knew it had come from her.'

'That must have been so hard,' I said, my heart breaking at the thought of Martin forcing Helen to cut contact with her parents.

'It was,' she sighed. 'We hoped that one day she would change her mind and get back in touch.

'We were so worried, but she was a grown woman and had made a life for herself in another country. I couldn't understand what we'd done but I think Claude and I knew that it was all coming from Martin. He simply didn't want to share her with anyone else.'

She started to cry.

'It's heartbreaking to think of what she was going through and how he was treating her. Helen is such a gentle, kind soul and she was practically a prisoner in that house. If only we'd known. If only we'd tried harder to get back in touch, maybe things could have turned out differently.'

I put my hand on hers to try to offer her some comfort.

'I'm so sorry,' I said. 'I didn't mean to upset you.'

'Not at all,' she smiled. 'There's been a lot of tears over the past few months. We're just hoping that the judge will be lenient with Helen when they know what she's been through. In the meantime, we're making up for lost time and enjoying having our daughter and granddaughter back in our lives. Nancy seems like such a lovely girl.'

'She really is,' I told her. 'She's been through so much but she's doing well.'

It was awful to know that Martin's actions had impacted so many lives.

Just then, Juliet came back with Sid.

'I think somebody wants an ice cream,' she said, grinning.

'Have you been a good boy?' I asked him and he nodded.

'Can I have a lolly pease, Maggie?' he asked.

'Go on then,' I smiled.

'I'll go and get them,' said Marie. 'I bet Claude and Nancy will want one too.'

She wandered over to where the pair of them were messing about on the swings.

'How's it going?' asked Juliet.

'It seems to be going really well,' I told her.

'They're a lovely couple,' she smiled. 'They wanted to see how today went but they really want to look at the possibility of having Nancy full-time.'

'Really?' I asked. 'Do they want to take her to France?'

'Not necessarily,' she said. 'If this meeting went well and both they and Nancy are happy then they would be prepared to stay in the UK.'

She'd already checked with Helen and she was delighted with the idea and was happy for them to live in her old house.

'Obviously, it's still very early days,' she told me. 'Nancy might not be keen on the idea, and we'd have to do all the checks and things.'

It was a bit of a shock for me but as I looked over at Nancy, happily tucking into an ice cream and chatting away to her granny and grandpa, I was full of hope that this could really work. In fact, it might be the ideal solution.

CHAPTER EIGHTEEN

Coming Home

Soon it was time to head back home. Sid was getting tired and needed lunch and we'd been at the park for nearly two hours which I thought was long enough for a first meeting.

As Nancy said goodbye, Juliet had a quiet word with me.

'I'll come back to your house, Maggie, if that's OK?' she asked. 'I'd like to have a quick chat to Nancy.'

Unprompted, Nancy ran over to Marie and Claude and gave them a hug goodbye. I could see that they were thrilled.

'It was so lovely to meet you,' Claude told her again.

'Thank you for playing with me, Grandpa,' she smiled.

'It was an absolute pleasure,' he replied.

'If it's OK with you, Nancy, we'd really love to see you again,' Marie told her.

She looked over at Juliet uncertainly, as if she wasn't sure whether she was allowed to ask that question.

'Nancy and I will have a chat when we get back and hopefully we can work something out,' Juliet replied, smiling.

When we got home, I got some lunch sorted for Sid while Juliet and Nancy sat at the kitchen table.

'Well, how did that go?' Juliet asked her. 'Did you enjoy meeting your grandparents for the first time?'

Nancy nodded.

'They were really nice,' she smiled. 'Grandpa was really funny and Granny was kind and she reminded me of Mummy lots. Where do they live? I forgot to ask them.'

'Well, as you know, they normally live in France,' explained Juliet. 'But while they're over here in the UK, Mummy said they could stay in your old house.'

'My house?' she asked, looking confused. 'The one that me, Mummy and Daddy lived in?'

'Yes,' nodded Juliet. 'Hotels cost lots of money and the house was empty so your mum suggested they stay there.'

'I suppose they can keep it nice and tidy for when Mummy comes home,' she shrugged. 'When can I see them again?' she asked.

Juliet explained that Marie had had an idea.

'How would you feel about going round to your old house to have dinner with them one night after school?'

Nancy looked unsure.

'It might feel a bit strange without Mummy and Daddy there but I'd like to see my old bedroom and all of my things.' She hesitated. 'Can Maggie come too?'

'Of course,' nodded Juliet. 'And Sid.'

'OK then,' she said.

I could tell she was pleased about seeing her grandparents again but nervous about going back to her old house. I wasn't surprised. The last time she'd been there she'd discovered her beloved father in a pool of blood on the kitchen floor.

So much had happened since then and she'd been through a lot, so I understood why she was hesitant. I knew it might be quite traumatic and emotional for her.

Three days later, with Sid strapped in the back in his car seat, we picked up Nancy from school.

'Are you looking forward to seeing Granny and Grandpa?' I asked her.

She nodded but I could see she was apprehensive.

I'd just turned off the main road and was heading towards the leafy street where her house was, when Nancy turned to me.

'I don't want to go. I don't want to go, Maggie. I want to go back to your house. Please,' she begged. 'Can we go back now?'

I could see how distressed she was, so I pulled over.

'It's OK, flower,' I told her. 'You're just panicking. What are you worried about?'

'I don't want to go to my old house,' she replied. 'I don't want to go in the kitchen and see Daddy's blood all over the floor. It will make me too sad. I don't want to see it, Maggie.'

The poor child had got herself into such a state and it was horrible to see her so distressed.

'There won't be any blood on the kitchen floor, sweetie,' I reassured her. 'After Daddy died, the house was all cleaned up and Granny and Grandpa will have made sure that it's all clean and tidy.'

'But what if you can still see the red marks on the floor, Maggie?'

'It will be absolutely fine,' I reassured her. 'If it makes you feel any better, then I can go into the kitchen first and check for you?'

'It's OK,' she sighed but I could she see that she was really shaken up.

'If you really don't want to go to your old house, Nancy, then you don't have to,' I told her. 'You don't have to see your grandparents either.'

'I want to,' she replied. 'I want to see them and I want to go back to the house.'

'Shall I start the car again?' I asked her and she nodded.

'I know you're feeling worried and I know it's going to be strange being in the house where you lived with Mummy and Daddy and them not being there, but it will be OK.'

For Nancy's sake, I truly hoped that I was right.

Five minutes later, we pulled up outside the huge detached house. The front gates were open so I drove in. I got Sid out of his car seat but Nancy was still sitting there, not moving.

I opened the passenger door for her.

'Do you still want to go in?' I asked her.

She nodded bravely.

I knocked on the door and Marie came to open it.

'Hello,' she beamed as she saw the three of us standing there. 'Come on in.'

Claude was waiting in the hallway. He chatted to Nancy while I had a quiet word with Marie.

'I think Nancy's feeling a bit strange about being back here,' I told her.

'The poor love,' she sighed. 'I did wonder if it might all be a bit much for her but Juliet said she might enjoy seeing her old things.'

Nancy did seem to be excited to be back as she ran in and out of the rooms on the ground floor. But she paused when she got to the kitchen.

'Do you want to come through with me and have a glass of juice?' Marie said, holding out her hand to her. Nancy took it and I followed them in.

The kitchen was huge and modern with large doors overlooking the garden. Nancy looked around nervously and I could see her staring at the floor. Thankfully everything looked gleaming and immaculate.

'Oh, you've changed things around,' she gasped.

'Yes, we moved the table closer to the doors and the sofa over here,' Marie told her. 'Grandpa likes to do his crossword and chat to me while I cook so it works well.'

'It looks nice like this,' she said and she seemed a lot more reassured. 'I like that it's different.'

'Maggie, would you like to see upstairs?' she asked me. 'I can show you my bedroom if you want?'

'Yes, we'd like that lots, wouldn't we, Sid?' and he grinned before running up the stairs.

Nancy quickly ran up after him and she seemed delighted to be back as she looked around.

'That door's my bathroom,' she said excitedly. 'That's the other bathroom over there.'

She took me into one of the three spare bedrooms where she was surprised to see some suitcases on the floor and clothes hanging up.

'Oh, this must be where Granny and Grandpa are sleeping,' she said.

She stopped outside one of the doors.

'This is Mummy and Daddy's bedroom,' she said sadly. 'But I don't want to go in there.'

She pointed down the landing.

'And that's Daddy's office.'

Everywhere in the house must have held many memories for her. There was a huge photograph hanging on the landing wall of Helen, Martin and Nancy. I could tell it had been taken downstairs in the living room, the three of them were sitting on a huge grey velvet sofa with their arms around each other. They had big smiles on their faces and they looked like the perfect family. Nancy stared at it.

'I know Daddy was a bad man but I still miss him and I'm sad that he's dead,' she sighed.

'I know, lovey,' I told her. 'You can love someone but still not like the way they behave or treat other people.'

Nancy nodded sadly.

'Now, come on, why don't you show me your bedroom?' I asked her.

Nancy ran in and excitedly showed me and Sid round. It was exactly as Juliet had described it to me all those months ago when Nancy had first arrived at my house. It was the perfect little girl's bedroom and she had everything.

She showed me the rows of books, her favourite dresses that were still hanging in the wardrobes and the mountains of cuddly toys. I could see that she was thrilled to see all of her old things.

'Why don't you stay here and I'll go back downstairs and chat to Claude and Marie,' I said to her.

I wandered back downstairs. Marie sat on the floor and did a puzzle with Sid while Claude put the finishing touches on some pasta.

'How is she?' he asked.

'She seems fine,' I shrugged. 'I think she was a little bit

apprehensive and upset at first but she's OK now. She's enjoying being back in her bedroom.'

'She's such a sweetheart,' sighed Marie. 'I'm so impressed with how resilient she is.'

'Juliet mentioned that you'd like to take her full-time,' I said.

'Yes,' nodded Claude. 'I know it's early days and we need time to get to know each other properly but ultimately, she's family. We've already missed out on so much of her life, and we don't want to miss any more. Helen is happy with the idea but I know Social Services have to do all their checks and once we know that it can happen, Nancy has to be happy too.'

'How would you feel about that?' Marie asked. 'We wouldn't want to offend you, Maggie, and I can tell Nancy is happy at your house.'

'Nancy is a lovely girl and I'm very fond of her,' I told them, 'but I think that it would be wonderful for her to be able to live with you both. She's been through so much, and more than anything she deserves to be happy. If she's on board with coming to live with you both, then I am too.'

I meant every word. I would have happily given Nancy a long-term home but when a child can be taken in by relatives, it's often the best solution.

'Are you thinking of taking her back to France?' I asked.

Claude shook his head.

'No, she's had so much upheaval in her life in the past few months, we think it's better for her to stay in school and be near Helen.'

'None of us know what's going to happen with the court case, but I think Helen's going to be in prison for a while,' sighed Marie. 'Nancy's going to need a lot of support and I think it's important that she visits her mama and maintains contact.'

I was full of admiration for them that they were both willing to give up their lives and jobs in France and move over here to look after Nancy.

A few minutes later, Nancy came back downstairs so there was no more talk of moving. We had a lovely dinner and afterwards we all played a game of dominoes.

'We have to get back, sweetie, as I need to put Sid to bed,' I told her once we'd finished the game.

'Aww,' she sighed. 'I wanted to go back in my old bedroom for a bit.'

'Well, we'll talk to Juliet and see if you can come back another time,' Claude told her.

While Nancy gave Claude a hug, Marie was showing Sid how to tie the laces on his shoes.

'Look, you make two loops like bunny ears then you tie them in a knot,' she explained patiently.

'Oh, that's how Mummy taught me,' smiled Nancy.

'That's because it's how I taught your mama to do it too,' Marie told her.

After more hugs goodbye, we headed home.

'How was that?' I asked her. 'How did you feel being back in your house?'

'It was a bit weird and sad but nice too,' she sighed. 'I really liked seeing my old bedroom.'

'Maybe the next time you could see Granny and Grandpa on your own?' I suggested and Nancy seemed to like that idea.

I had a chat with Juliet, who agreed that it would be fine for Nancy to spend time with Marie and Claude, so the following weekend, Sid and I dropped her off in the morning and she spent the day there with them. After tea, I picked her up.

As we drove her home, she was much quieter than usual.

'Did you have a good day, flower?' I asked her and she nodded, then she hesitated as though she was waiting to say something.

'Maggie, you know how Granny and Grandpa are living in my old house?'

'Yes,' I said.

'Do you think I could go there one day and live with them?'

'Would you like that?' I asked her and she nodded firmly.

'I really like living with you and Sid, Maggie, but I miss my old bedroom and being close to school and not having to wake up so early. And all my old things are there and I think Mummy would like us all to live together too.'

'I think that sounds like a great idea,' I smiled. 'But what we really need to do is talk to Juliet about it.'

'OK,' she said. 'Can you ring her tomorrow?'

'Well tomorrow's Sunday, lovey, but I promise that I will speak to her first thing on Monday morning.'

I kept my word and on Monday, I called Juliet and told her what Nancy had said.

'She actually suggested it herself,' I laughed. 'Now I've just got everything crossed that it will happen.'

'At this stage it's looking very promising,' Juliet told me.

Helen had given her permission for Nancy to live with her grandparents, and in France, Marie and Claude had both worked with children. Claude was a maths teacher and Marie ran after-school sewing clubs, so they both had the French equivalent of DBS checks and they'd passed the police checks in the UK.

'I'll come round and talk to Nancy tonight,' she told me.

After so much bad news, for once it was a visit of Juliet's that I was looking forward to.

When Nancy opened the door and saw Juliet standing there, she eyed her suspiciously.

'What is it?' she asked her.

'Well, if you let me come in, I can tell you,' she smiled.

We all sat in the kitchen so I could keep an eye on Sid who was playing outside in the sandpit.

'Maggie told me that you'd like to go and live with your grandparents,' she said, and Nancy nodded. 'Funnily enough your granny and grandpa have been asking me exactly the same thing and your mum is happy with the idea too.'

'Really?' she smiled.

'And you wouldn't mind, Maggie?' she asked me. 'You wouldn't be too sad if I left?'

'I'd miss you a lot, but I think it would be lovely for you to be able to live in your old house with your family,' I told her. 'And besides, I've got Sid here to keep me company.'

Nancy couldn't stop smiling.

'When can I go?' she asked.

'Well you've only got two weeks of school left so you can carry on going to school from here but you can stay with Granny and Grandpa at the weekends. Then, when it's the summer holidays, you can move back properly and live there full-time.'

'And then when Mummy comes out of prison, she can live with us all too,' Nancy smiled.

Juliet and I looked at each other.

'Remember we don't know when that's going to be though, lovey,' I reminded her gently. 'Mummy still has to go to court and she could be staying in prison for many years.'

'I know,' she sighed.

Even though I'd be sad to say goodbye to Nancy after everything that had happened, I knew in my heart that it was the ideal solution for her, and that it would be in her best interests.

Over the next couple of weeks, she spent weekends with Marie and Claude at her old house as well as staying overnight a couple of times in the week. She didn't have much stuff at my house but each time she went, she took a few more things with her.

Rather than having the usual big, emotional goodbye, which I didn't think was very helpful for children, it all felt very relaxed and gradual.

Nancy's last day at my house was a Saturday, and in the morning Louisa and Charlie popped round.

'I'm so sad to say goodbye to Edie,' sighed Nancy as she gave her a hug.

'It's not really goodbye though,' Louisa told her. 'I'm sure we'll bump into you at the park and you're welcome to come round and see her anytime you like.'

'Yes,' smiled Nancy. 'And I could push Edie on the swings like I do with Sid.'

'I bet she'll love that when she's big enough,' Louisa replied, smiling.

After saying goodbye, they were going to go for a walk. Louisa put Edie back into her pram and Charlie handed her a blanket.

'Don't forget to put this on her,' he told her.

'I'm not going to put a blanket on her in this weather,' she replied. 'It's boiling out there.'

As Charlie shrugged and put the blanket under the pram, I could see Nancy watching them intently.

As we waved them off down the street, she turned to me.

'Will Louisa get into trouble for not doing what Charlie said?' she asked me.

'What did she do?' I asked, puzzled.

She explained how she'd refused to put the blanket on Edie.

'She didn't do anything wrong lovey,' I told her. 'That's just normal conversation between two parents. Louisa was expressing her opinion and Charlie listened to what she thought. She won't be in trouble. It's OK for people to disagree on things, and it doesn't mean that anyone has to get cross.'

I could see her taking it all in and I couldn't help but be reminded of how different things must have been at her house.

After Charlie, Louisa and Edie had left, we put the last of her things in the car and Sid and I drove her over to her old house. Claude and Marie had invited us to stay for lunch.

It felt like a normal day rather than a big farewell, which was exactly how I wanted it to be. After we'd eaten, Nancy took Sid into the garden.

'It's going to be a tough few months,' sighed Claude. 'The court hearing is coming up and Nancy is going to need a lot of help and support going forwards.'

'I really hope that we get it right,' added Marie.

'You will,' I reassured them. 'Nancy is working through things in her own mind so all you can do is answer her questions honestly and openly when she asks them.'

I explained how I thought the most useful thing for Nancy would be having the stability of living with them. It would enable her to see how a loving, equal marriage worked.

'We're definitely not perfect,' laughed Marie. 'We have our arguments and disagreements.'

'But that's completely normal,' I told her.

They were also going to visit Helen every week in prison.

'We don't want Nancy to miss too much school so I think we'll take her once a month,' said Claude.

After a couple of hours, I knew it was time to head back as Jo was going to call in later to see Sid.

'Saying goodbye to children must be one of the hardest parts of fostering,' smiled Marie.

'It is,' I sighed. 'It's something you never get used to, no matter how many times you've done it. But when you know a child is moving on to a place where they're secure and happy, it makes it a lot easier.'

Marie called Nancy in from the garden.

'Maggie and Sid have got to go now, ma cherie,' she told her.

Nancy looked close to tears as she picked Sid up and gave him a hug.

'Bye Siddy,' she told him. 'I hope I see you again soon.'

'He's really going to miss you,' I told her. 'Thank you for being so brilliant with him.'

Then it was my turn for a cuddle.

'Bye bye, flower,' I smiled. 'I'm not going to be sad because I know you're going to be well looked after here.'

I promised to keep in touch and call in from time to time.

'I want to know how things go with Mummy at court,'

I told her. 'And you've got my phone number if you ever want to chat or come round for dinner.'

'And you're welcome here any time, Maggie,' Marie told me.

Even though I knew it was the best possible solution for Nancy, I still had a lump in my throat as I strapped Sid into his car seat.

I willed myself not to cry and I turned and gave her one last cheery wave. But as I pulled out of the driveway and on to the road, I let the tears fall.

'I'm a big old softie aren't I, Sid?' I smiled as we headed home.

Sid giggled, without a care in the world, and his gorgeous little face lifted my spirits.

I was grateful I had him to look after for a few more weeks. I knew he would keep me busy and make the house feel less empty.

It's a lovely feeling when a child goes to live with relatives and I knew it was the right thing for Nancy. She'd been through so much trauma in her young life, but being back in her old house with her grandparents would give her the stability and familiarity to help her get through the next few years.

It was going to take her a long time to truly understand why Helen had been driven to do what she did and perhaps she never would. But I hoped that, with Marie and Claude's love and support, she would eventually learn to forgive her mother and they could move on with their lives together.

CHAPTER NINETEEN

Facing the Future

Four Months Later

Before I got out of the car, I checked my reflection in the driver's mirror one last time. I smoothed my hair down and put a bit of lip balm on.

'Come on, Maggie,' I told myself, taking a deep breath. 'You can do this.'

There was something about going to the Crown Court that always made me nervous, and ever since I'd got up today, my stomach hadn't stopped churning.

I quickly grabbed my handbag, got out of the car and walked through the car park and on to the main road. I could see two figures ahead of me, standing waiting outside the entrance to the court.

Claude and Marie.

As I got closer to them, I could see how nervous and apprehensive they looked.

Claude gave me a smile and leant over and kissed me on each cheek.

'Thanks so much for coming, Maggie.'

Marie did the same.

'It means so much to us to have you here,' she told me.

'I wanted to come,' I replied, meaning it. 'Both for Nancy's sake, and to support both of you, and Helen as well.'

It felt like the last piece of the puzzle and a way of bringing closure. Since Nancy had left my house, the criminal investigation into Martin's death had been ongoing.

After Helen's confession about how Martin had treated her, her legal team had found both Martin's logbook and Helen's diary hidden at the house. Their content dated back years, and both had apparently made equally harrowing reading. Due to this new evidence, the Crown Prosecution Service (CPS) had agreed to reduce the charges from murder to manslaughter with diminished responsibility, and Helen had pleaded guilty. It had been a huge relief to Claude and Marie and, of course, Nancy, that she wasn't facing a murder charge. But manslaughter could still carry a custodial sentence of up to ten years, and now they still had to prepare themselves for the very real possibility that Helen was going to have to stay in prison for a significant amount of time.

Today, we'd come to the Crown Court to see Helen being sentenced.

'How's Nancy holding up?' I asked them.

It had been a couple of weeks since I'd last been round to Claude and Marie's house to have dinner with them and Nancy.

Claude shrugged his shoulders sadly.

'She's very up and down,' sighed Marie. 'She knows what's happening today and even though we've tried to reassure her, she's very frightened about what's going to happen to her mama.'

'That's understandable,' I sighed. 'It must be so hard for her.'

'She wanted to come but we didn't think it was appropriate,' added Claude. 'I think it would have been too much for her. We thought she should go to school as normal, and we're hoping it'll be a bit of a distraction.'

'I think you're right,' I said. 'It would have been really harrowing for her.'

Although I felt it was important that Nancy be able to get closure on everything that had happened, my personal view was that courts weren't appropriate places for young children.

'And how's Helen doing?' I asked.

'She's completely terrified,' said Marie, her eyes filling with tears. 'She just doesn't know what to expect. She knows that realistically she's going to have to stay in prison, but she's worried they're going to lock her up and throw away the key. She's not sleeping, and she's barely been eating. She's also worried they're going to send her to a prison at the other end of the country so it would be difficult for us to see her.'

My heart went out to Helen. The few times I'd met her in prison she'd seemed so fragile and frail and, from hearing what life had been like with Martin, she had been through so much. All we could do was hope that the judge was going to be fair.

'We'd better go in,' said Claude, suddenly looking at his watch.

'No sign of Juliet yet?' I asked.

'Oh, she's already in there,' replied Marie. 'She went in earlier with Helen's solicitor, Amanda.'

'Right then,' I smiled. 'Let's go.'

I felt nervous, but I couldn't begin to imagine what they were feeling at that moment, waiting to watch their daughter go up in front of a judge who held the key to her freedom.

Going into a Crown Court was always a bit of a palaver. This one was a huge, modern building with a big glass reception. It was like being at the airport, and we had to put our bags into a tray to be scanned and then walk through a security arch. It was just before 10 a.m. and as most cases started at a similar time, the queue was huge.

Finally it was our turn. Claude emptied his pockets into a tray and then walked through the arch, then Marie and I did the same. A screen on the wall told us which court Helen's sentencing was in.

'Oh no, it's a man,' sighed Marie looking at the name of the judge and the photograph next to it. *The Hon. Justice Higgins.* 'I thought a woman might be more sympathetic to what Helen had been through somehow,' she sighed.

'It doesn't matter,' Claude told her, giving her hand a squeeze. 'He's got all the reports. He'll see what Helen's life was like.'

We got a lift up to the second floor to the courtroom where the sentencing was taking place. As we pushed open the heavy door, I saw Juliet sitting in the public gallery and we went over and joined her. She and I made small talk as we waited for everything to get started, but Claude and Marie didn't say a word, they just sat in silence, squeezing each other's hands tightly.

As it was a sentencing rather than a trial, there weren't many people in the court. There was no need for a jury, so there were just a couple of court clerks, a defence and a prosecution barrister and just the judge to come.

'Who are they?' whispered Claude, pointing to a couple of men in their twenties and a slightly older woman sitting on some seats to the left of us.

'I think that's the press bench, so they're probably newspaper reporters,' replied Juliet.

The case had been widely covered in the press at the time of Martin's death and when Helen had gone missing. I knew how hard it must be for the family to have their personal lives broadcast so publicly, and to have so little control over what was written about them.

Our attention was suddenly diverted to the other side of the court, where Helen was led into the dock flanked by two uniformed security guards. I hadn't seen her for four months and I was shocked by how frail she looked. She was wearing a smart black dress but it hung off her gaunt frame, and her face looked hollow and drawn. She still had that vague, numb look in her eyes, as though she wasn't fully present. She looked up at the public gallery and when she saw Claude and Marie, she gave them a weak smile.

I could see Marie's eyes fill with tears at the sight of her vulnerable daughter and Claude grabbed her hand.

'It's OK,' he whispered to her. 'Whatever happens, we'll get through it.'

Suddenly the court clerk stood up and bustled up to the front of the court.

'All rise please,' she asked.

We all stood up as Justice Higgins came in. It was hard to tell his true age with his wig on but he was a serious-looking man.

Even though it was a sentencing, the prosecution still had to summarise its case. The prosecution barrister, a well-spoken woman, stood up and told the judge the circumstances around Martin's death. Even though I knew what had happened, it was still hard to hear about how Nancy had found him with the knife sticking out of his side.

'The defendant killed her husband and left him in a pool of his own blood on the kitchen floor of their home before she absconded,' the prosecution barrister said. 'She was on the run for several days before she was arrested at Dover trying to get on a ferry to see her family in France.'

In the dock, Helen stared resolutely at the floor and even from where we were sat, I could see that she was trembling. She was still wearing her wedding ring and as the prosecutor spoke, she twiddled it nervously around her finger.

After the Crown Prosecution Service (CPS) had quickly summarised the case, it was time for Helen's barrister to speak.

'It's clear from both her own diary and Martin Miller's logbook that Helen Miller was subjected to prolonged psychological abuse,' he told the court. 'For years, she was constantly humiliated, degraded and dehumanised. The final straw came when Martin Miller found her "escape money" and took it, therefore ending any chance that she and her young daughter had of leaving the marital home and breaking the control he had over them both.'

He also described how Martin had threatened to rape and kill Helen and harm Nancy too. In the dock, Helen started to sob and one of the security guards handed her a tissue.

'Your Honour, that night, Helen Miller had simply reached breaking point,' her barrister told him. 'After years of appalling psychological abuse and control, Martin Miller had taken away her only chance of escape, threatened her and her daughter, pinned her to the work surface and she believed he was about to force himself on her sexually. At that point in time, grabbing the knife seemed like the only viable option open to her. It was, she believed, the only way that she could escape the constant mental torment.'

A psychological assessment had also been submitted to the court which showed that Helen was suffering from severe depression and acute Post Traumatic Stress Disorder, brought on by years of emotional abuse.

Even though I already knew some of this, it was still absolutely harrowing to hear.

That poor woman.

I also thought of Nancy, and how she'd grown up witnessing this torture, thinking it was normal.

Then it was the judge's turn to speak.

'Will the defendant please stand in the dock,' the court clerk told her.

Helen looked terrified as she got to her feet. She looked like she could collapse at any minute and I could see her whole body trembling as she held on to the sides of the dock for support.

I could feel Marie tense up next to me and Claude squeezed her hand.

'I've heard and read both of your submissions as well as the pre-sentence report,' he said. 'Helen Miller, it's clear that for all of your married life together, Martin Miller exhibited a sense of ownership and entitlement over you. From both the harrowing entries in your diary and your husband's own recordings in his logbook, I can see that he isolated you from your family, monitored your time and movements and constantly put you down in the most degrading of ways. I can also see that you were suffering from a number of psychological conditions at the time of the offence.'

He paused and looked up at her over his glasses.

'However, nothing can take away from the fact that you took Martin Miller's life and then absconded from the scene until you were arrested several days later leaving your young daughter in the house to discover his body.'

At the mention of Nancy, Helen covered her mouth with her hand and let out a whimper.

'I'm satisfied that you're not a danger to the general public and your risk of reoffending is low but the seriousness of this crime must be reflected in a custodial sentence.'

I swallowed the lump in my throat.

Please for Nancy's sake, don't lock her up for ten years, I willed.

Neither of them deserved that and Nancy desperately needed her mum around her to help make sense of what they'd been through and how Martin had treated them.

In the bench next to me, Claude shut his eyes and Marie looked terrified.

The judge continued.

'For the crime of manslaughter on the grounds of diminished responsibility, I sentence you to five years in prison.'

In the dock, Helen keeled over and started to sob. She looked up at the public gallery.

'I'm sorry,' she whimpered to Claude and Marie. 'Tell Nancy I'm so, so sorry and that I love her.'

'It's OK, darling,' Marie called out to her. 'We'll get through this. You'll be OK.'

But as a terrified-looking Helen was led back down to the cells, Marie collapsed into Claude's arms and sobbed.

Five years.

To be honest, I didn't know what to think. It was better than ten but it didn't feel like anything to celebrate. Nancy was going to spend most of her early teenage years without her mother by her side.

Juliet turned to Claude and Marie.

'We'll talk to her solicitor Amanda but hopefully with good behaviour she will be out after three years.'

But to them, it was still understandably devastating. As we walked out of the court, my heart felt heavy.

'We need to go and get Nancy,' sighed Claude. 'We promised to go and pick her up from school once we knew.'

'Do you want me to come with you and help break the news?' asked Juliet.

Marie shook her head.

'Thank you but I think we need to do this on our own,' she told her.

I didn't envy them. Nancy had been through so much in the past six months and I wasn't sure how she was going to take this news.

'If there's anything I can do then let me know,' I told them.

'We will do,' Marie told me.

She wrapped her arms around me and gave me a hug.

'Thank you so much for coming, Maggie,' she told me. 'We really appreciate it and everything you've done for Nancy,' added Claude, squeezing my hand.

'I wanted to be here,' I smiled.

As I headed back to the car, I just felt flat and exhausted.

I turned on my phone to a flurry of texts. One from Louisa, one from my friend Vicky and also a message from Becky, all asking how the sentencing had gone.

She got five years, I typed. *The family are devastated.*

Whether she served the full five or three, those years were going to feel like a lifetime to Helen, Nancy and her grand parents. Yes, she'd taken a man's life, and she needed to be punished for that, but I had seen for myself how she'd been driven to the brink by living with that monster.

Before I set off for home, I sent my boyfriend Graham a quick text.

Have you got time to grab a quick bite to eat with me tonight? I could do with the company x

I knew he was busy at work but I didn't want to spend the rest of the day at home on my own. I thought it would help to see someone else and be distracted for a few hours.

I wasn't fostering any children currently, and the house felt horribly quiet when I arrived back. Little Sid had finally gone home after Fred was released from hospital a couple of months ago, and I missed his joyful little smile. Jo kept in touch from time to time and I was delighted to hear that they were all doing well and the number of seizures Fred was having had dramatically reduced since his surgery. Since then, I'd had a few temporary emergency placements and a few weeks of respite care, but right now it was just me rattling around the house on my own. I didn't mind too much, as it meant I could spend lots of time with Louisa and Edie, who was getting bigger by the day and changing every time that I saw her. Louisa was thriving as a mum, and spending time with my beautiful granddaughter gave me so much pleasure.

*

A couple of days later, I got a text from Marie.

We'd really like it if you could come round for dinner at the house. Nancy would love to see you.

Of course, I replied.

I was keen to see her and check how she was getting on after the sentencing.

When I arrived at the house one evening a few days later, Marie opened the door with Nancy by her side.

'Maggie!' grinned Nancy, throwing her arms around me. 'Did you bring Louisa and Edie?'

'No flower, I'm afraid it's just me,' I told her. 'Baby Edie will be at home asleep right now, as it's long past her bedtime.'

Thankfully, Nancy seemed very chirpy. She was desperate to show me her bedroom and the hamster Claude and Marie had bought her that she'd called Squeaky, and after a quick greeting with Claude and Marie, she hurried me upstairs to show me around.

'Daddy wouldn't let us have any pets,' she told me as she showed me his cage and the tunnels that he liked to play in.

She paused at the mention of her dad.

'Even though my dad was a bad person, sometimes I still miss him,' she sighed.

'I know you do, sweetie,' I told her. 'And that's completely understandable. No matter what he did, he's still your dad.'

Nancy suddenly looked sad.

'Did you know that Mummy has to stay in prison for a very long time?' she told me and I nodded.

'I know,' I sighed. 'I'm so sorry, Nancy.'

'It's OK,' she said. 'I can still go and visit her and Granny and Grandpa said if she's really good then she might be able to come home in three years. Then I'll only be fourteen,' she smiled.

I was suddenly struck by what a brave and resilient girl she was. Despite everything that she and Helen had been through and the horrendous things that had happened, I knew that she would be OK. Nancy was having regular counselling and with Claude and Marie's help, I knew she was going to receive the love and support she needed to be able to get through the next few years. And then one day, for the first time ever, she and Helen would finally be free to live their lives in the way they wanted to. We all had to hold on to that hope.

Epilogue

What Helen's case taught me was that domestic abuse isn't always physical. What she and Nancy had been through showed that emotional or psychological abuse can be just as damaging as physical abuse, and that even if there weren't any actual scars that could be seen, the harm it caused inside was every bit as damaging. As a foster carer, I'd done many courses on domestic violence. I knew how to spot it and help people and families who have experienced it. The emotional abuse suffered by Helen at her husband's hands had proved almost impossible to detect from the outside but it proved to be every bit as devastating as physical violence.

Thankfully now, many years after I fostered Nancy, we know a lot more about what's now known as coercive control. Sadly, it's taken several high-profile cases of women, just like Helen, killing their partners, or women being killed by their partners to finally make coercive control a criminal offence in its own right.

According to Women's Aid, coercive control is an act or a pattern of acts of assault, threats, humiliation and intimidation or other abuse that is used to harm, punish or frighten the victim. This controlling behaviour is designed to make a person dependent by isolating them from support, exploiting them, depriving them of independence and regulating their everyday behaviour. Experts liken it to being taken hostage.

I kept in touch with Nancy over the years, and she blossomed into a beautiful, intelligent and kind young woman. As she got older, though, she still struggled to understand her past and the conflicting feelings she had towards her parents. Even after Helen was released from prison after serving just over three years of her five year sentence, her life was never the same after what she had been through. Both Nancy and Helen wanted me to tell their story in the hope that it might help another person reading it to recognise what they were going through and seek help.

If you think that you or someone you know is in a controlling relationship then please go to womensaid.org.uk for help, support and advice.

A Note from Maggie

I really hope you enjoyed reading this story. I love sharing my experiences of fostering with you, and I also love hearing what you think about them. If you enjoyed this book, or any of my others, please think about leaving a review online. I know other readers really benefit from your thoughts, and I do too.

To be the first to hear about my new books, you can keep in touch on my Facebook page @MaggieHartleyAuthor. I find it inspiring to learn about your own experiences of fostering and adoption, and to read your comments and reviews.

Finally, thank you so much for choosing to read *Behind Closed Doors*. If you enjoyed it, there are others available including *A Sister's Shame*; *Too Scared to Cry*; *Tiny Prisoners*; *The Little Ghost Girl*; *A Family for Christmas*; *Too Young to be a Mum, Who Will Love Me Now? The Girl No One Wanted*; *Battered, Broken, Healed*; *Sold to be a Wife*; *Denied a Mummy*; *Daddy's Little Soldier* and *Please, Don't Take My Sisters*. I hope you'll enjoy my next story just as much.

Maggie Hartley

Acknowledgements

Thank you to my children, Tess, Pete and Sam who are such a big part of my fostering today even though I had not met you when Nancy came into my home. To my wide circle of fostering friends – you know who you are! Your support and your laughter are valued. To my friend Andrew B for your continued encouragement and care. Thanks also to Heather Bishop who spent many hours listening and enabled this story to be told, my literary agent Rowan Lawton and to Anna Valentine and Marleigh Price at Seven Dials for giving me the opportunity to share these stories.

CREDITS

Maggie Hartley and Seven Dials would like to thank everyone at Orion who worked on the publication of *Behind Closed Doors*.

Agent
Rowan Lawton

Editors
Marleigh Price
Ru Merritt

Copy-editor
Clare Wallis

Proofreader
Elise See Tai

Editorial Management
Jane Hughes
Charlie Panayiotou
Tamara Morriss
Claire Boyle

Audio
Paul Stark
Jake Alderson
Georgina Cutler

Contracts
Anne Goddard
Ellie Bowker
Humayra Ahmed

Design
Nick Shah
[DESIGNER]
Joanna Ridley
Helen Ewing

Finance
Nick Gibson
Jasdip Nandra
Elizabeth Beaumont
Ibukun Ademefun
Afeera Ahmed
Sue Baker
Tom Costello

Inventory
Jo Jacobs
Dan Stevens

Marketing
Lucy Cameron

Production
Claire Keep
Fiona McIntosh

Publicity
Patricia Deever

Sales
Jen Wilson
Victoria Laws
Esther Waters
Frances Doyle
Ben Goddard
Jack Hallam
Anna Egelstaff
Inês Figueira
Barbara Ronan
Andrew Hally
Dominic Smith
Deborah Deyong
Lauren Buck
Maggy Park
Linda McGregor
Sinead White
Jemimah James
Rachael Jones
Jack Dennison
Nigel Andrews
Ian Williamson
Julia Benson
Declan Kyle
Robert Mackenzie
Megan Smith
Charlotte Clay
Rebecca Cobbold

Operations

Sharon Willis

Rights

Susan Howe

Krystyna Kujawinska

Jessica Purdue

Ayesha Kinley

Louise Henderson

DADDY'S LITTLE SOLDIER

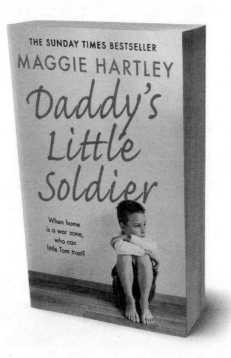

Tom has been taken into care following concerns that his dad is struggling to cope after the death of Tom's mum. When Maggie meets Tom's dad Mark, a stern ex-soldier and strict disciplinarian, it's clear that Tom's life at home without his mummy has been a constant battlefield. Can Maggie help Mark to raise a son and not a soldier? Or is little Tom going to lose his daddy too?

PLEASE, DON'T TAKE MY SISTERS

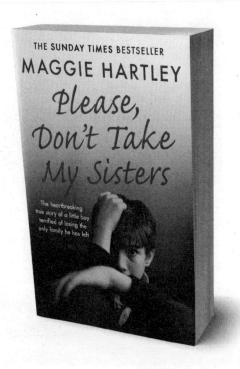

Leo's little sisters are the only family he has left in the world. But when Social Services begin to look at rehoming the little girls without their troubled older brother, the siblings' whole world comes crashing down. Can Maggie fight to keep the children together? Or will Leo lose the only love he's ever known?

A DESPERATE CRY FOR HELP

Meg arrives at Maggie's after a fire destroys the children's home she's been living in. But traumatised by the fire, and angry and vulnerable, having been put into care by her mother, Meg is lashing out at everyone around her. Can Maggie reach this damaged little girl before it's too late? And before Meg's destructive behaviour puts Maggie's life – and the lives of the other children in her care – at risk?

TINY PRISONERS

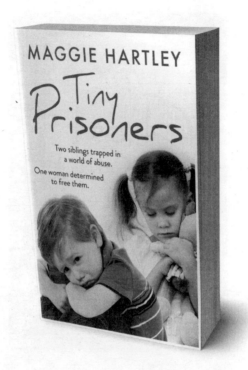

Evie and Elliot are scrawny, filthy and wide-eyed with fear when they turn up on foster carer Maggie Hartley's doorstep. They're too afraid to leave the house and any intrusion of the outside world sends them into a panic. It's up to Maggie to unlock the truth of their heart-breaking upbringing, and to help them learn to smile again.

THE LITTLE GHOST GIRL

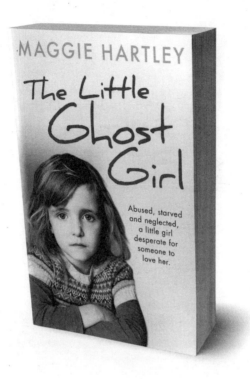

Ruth is a ghost of a girl when she arrives into foster mother Maggie Hartley's care. Pale, frail and withdrawn, it's clear to Maggie that Ruth had seen and experienced things that no 11-year-old should have to. Ruth is in desperate need of help, but can Maggie get through to her and unearth the harrowing secret she carries?

TOO YOUNG TO BE A MUM

When sixteen-year-old Jess arrives on foster carer Maggie Hartley's doorstep with her newborn son Jimmy, she has nowhere else to go. With social services threatening to take baby Jimmy into care, Jess knows that Maggie is her only chance of keeping her son. Can Maggie help Jess learn to become a mum?

WHO WILL LOVE ME NOW?

At just ten years old, Kirsty has already suffered a lifetime of heartache and suffering. When her latest foster carers decide they can no longer cope, Kirsty comes to live with Maggie. Reeling from this latest rejection, the young girl is violent and hostile, and Social Services fear that she may be a danger to those around her. Maggie finds herself in an impossible position, one that calls into question her decision to become a foster carer in the first place...

BATTERED, BROKEN, HEALED

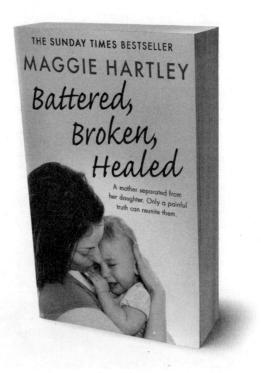

Six-week-old baby Jasmine comes to stay with Maggie after she is removed from her home. Neighbours have repeatedly called the police on suspicion of domestic violence, but her timid mother Hailey vehemently denies that anything is wrong. Can Maggie persuade Hailey to admit what's going on behind closed doors so that mother and baby can be reunited?

SOLD TO BE A WIFE

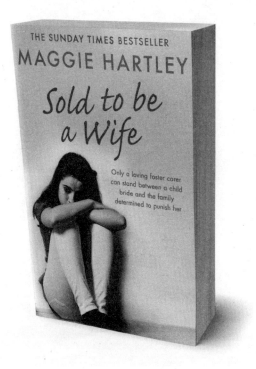

Fourteen-year-old Shazia has been taken into care over a fears that her family are planning to send her to Pakistan for an arranged marriage. But with Shazia denying everything and with social services unable to find any evidence, Shazia is eventually allowed to return home. But when Maggie wakes up a few weeks later in the middle of the night to a call from the terrified Shazia, it looks like her worst fears have been confirmed...

DENIED A MUMMY

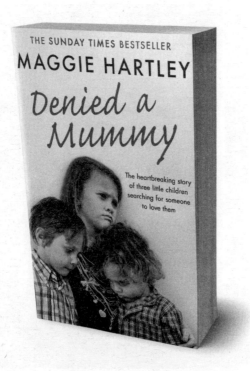

Maggie has her work cut out for her when her latest placement arrives on her doorstep; two little boys, aged five and seven and their eight- year-old sister. Having suffered extensive abuse and neglect, Maggie must slowly work through their trauma with love and care. But when a couple is approved to adopt the siblings, alarm bells start to ring. Maggie tries to put her own fears to one side but she can't shake the feeling of dread as she waves goodbye to them. Will these vulnerable children ever find a forever family?

TOO SCARED TO CRY

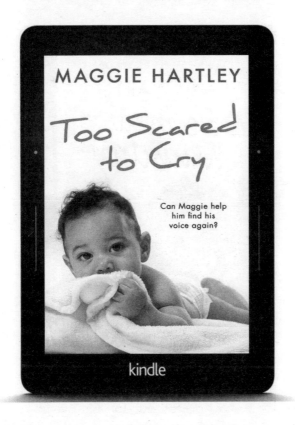

A baby too scared to cry. Two toddlers too scared to speak. This is the dramatic short story of three traumatised siblings, whose lives are transformed by the love of foster carer Maggie Hartley.

A FAMILY FOR CHRISTMAS

A tragic accident leaves the life of toddler Edward changed forever and his family wracked with guilt. Will Maggie be able to help this family grieve for the son they've lost and learn to love the little boy he is now? And will Edward have a family to go home to at Christmas?

THE GIRL NO ONE WANTED

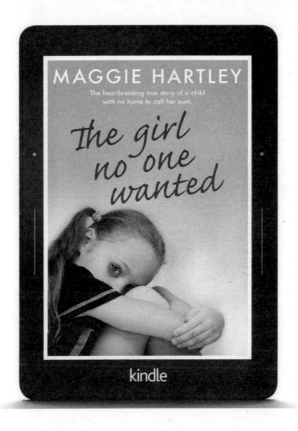

Eleven-year-old Leanne is out of control. With over forty placements in her short life, no local foster carers are willing to take in this angry and damaged little girl. Maggie is Leanne's only hope, and her last chance. If this placement fails, Leanne will have to be put in a secure unit. Where most others would simply walk away, Maggie refuses to give up on the little girl who's never known love.

IS IT MY FAULT MUMMY?

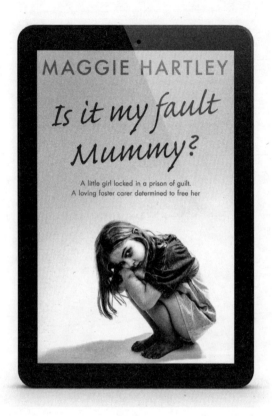

Seven-year-old Paris is trapped in a prison of guilt. Devastated after the death of her baby brother, Joel, Maggie faces one of the most heartbreaking cases yet as she tries to break down the wall of guilt surrounding this damaged little girl.

A SISTER'S SHAME

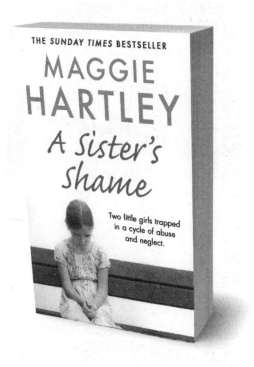

Nothing could prepare Maggie for the arrival of young sisters Billie and Bo. Subjected to unimaginable neglect, slowly the sisters begin to emerge from their shells but, as time goes on, it becomes clear something much darker is going on. Can Maggie unearth the secret behind their past? And can she help the sisters break free from their trauma?